One
Unity

AF192116

I like to dedicate this book to all species in existence today into eternity into infinity.

One
Unity
Now and beyond

By

Medusa D.B. Loveheart

The Last Warlock

~

Ancient Warlock
A New age Alchemist

FSC

www.fsc.org

MIX

Papper från
ansvarsfulla källor
Paper from
responsible sources

FSC® C105338

Book cover made by Lesia T. on fiverr.com

Third edition

© Medusa Loveheart 2024
Förlag: BoD · Books on Demand, Stockholm, Sverige
Tryck: Libri Plureos GmbH, Hamburg, Tyskland
ISBN: 978-91-8080-021-1

Attention!

This book might just demolish the future perspective
you have completely
that said please do enjoy the reading.

- Welcome back old friend. I see you returned from the wild. I assume you had a lot to process from the last book and yet you come visit me again. Bravo. Where were we... Oh yeah now I remember...

.

The New World Order

One Versa - One Planet - One Nation

Time as financial eco system

One Language

One Timeline - Year 0 again

One Law

We are all equally equipped with
Heart and Brain

Dao Buddhism as foundation of total
Normality Norm

True: Faith - Truth - Love -
Equality - Coexistence

...

.

- So, what does it mean and how
does it work?

.

We live in an old world today and it is not working
properly. The political climate is out of order and with
all the different perspective on the world of today it
is nearly impossible to achieve something greater of
existence. We can control our future and control our
planet if we just put our mind to it. We need to do a
complete reset of the way we think today and
embrace the possibilities of tomorrow. This step is
the biggest step in human mankind. This is the true
awakening happening, even if it does not happen
directly it will happen over time. If this world is
united, we will become more stronger and more
powerful than you can ever imagine. We need to
unite as one and still embrace our diversity to the
fullest. We need to start managing our resources so
that they last as long as possible and make sure we
always have enough to take our next step. By doing
this we will always have enough food for everyone
and always have some where to live and always be
able to direct our future in the best possible way
there is. For hundreds of thousands of years, we have
created our self without being aware about it. Now
it's time to take charge and gear our future in any
way we like. It is a natural step to take. From here on
it can go two ways. Either we end it all and screw up
or we shape up and do something about it.

- I think we both know what
direction we would like to choose.

It's time to shape up. Instead of being a leach that sucks the earth dry we must do a one hundred eighty grades turn and put a new mindset in our heads. It's time we become this planet caretakers and protector. We must wake up and realize we are the number one predator on this planet and that it is our responsibility to make sure this planet never dies or last as long as possible.

...

.

- This is about us taking the step to become a higher form of civilization.

.

We have bartered with goods for a long time now. First, we bartered with what we have, to get what we want then money came into the picture. Money solved a lot of hard issues with trading. It was not practical to trade with items when you not necessarily had what you needed to get what you wanted. And it was difficult to bring the correct item to the dealer to trade with what you wanted. Money solved all this and made commerce much easier. Money is a great invention for a period of time, but that time has now come to its end. Or at least closing into an end. Money now create a hinderance for us to move forward in great directions. In order for us to live in a world where we progress as smooth as possible, we need to live in a world where time is the currency we use. Because when we have time as currency, we control the amount by what we use over a whole planet. We plan and allocate resources after the whole population, and we make sure that we only use enough for us to have a great life. We will look at the planet as a resource and plan areas of each resource for us to use. We will plan so wildlife always exist in large enough areas over the world and we will provide areas for animal farming and vegetables farming enough for us to always have enough food to live a good and healthy life. We will allocate minerals and metals so that it lasts for us, and we can build as many houses as possible we like in the healthiest material. We plan city areas and nature areas so that we have our green planet forever. We join forces in research and use the healthiest electricity we can use, and we join the worlds forces in medicine to provide the most hi tech and modern healthcare we can possibly imagine. Without money we can start living a green and healthy life where cars run on electric power, and we put our focus to make electric driven cars as good as possible. We can start to manage continents after their nature and produce what they are great at. We can always choose the best alternative for nature when it comes to factory's because money is no longer a factor. We can build the greatest cities in the universe both on height and width. But we can't exhaust our resources. Everything has to be done with great control on resources. We have to be very clever and invest a lot of time into utilizing resources and make new ones. We must become experts in reusable resources and invest a lot of science into that. Which is not possible in a world of money? We would have a six-hour workday and twenty-four seven open so that everybody has a work to go to. We will re-educate our self with no problem in life so that we always can follow our heart. Food would be controlled on quota per week so that there is always enough for everyone. By keeping the world as one and distributing resources on the entire population we will have control over our resources. But we can't stop there we have to expand out into space and start managing resources on other planets as well. We have lots of renewable resources on earth, but some are limited and will deplete. We must be careful with those ones and manage them to last long enough for us to take the next step. We must start think big soon before it's too late.

...

.

- But there is a long way to go for this to happen.
- So how do we do it then.

.

Well, that's where Dao Buddhism comes into the picture. It's an ism that includes all, doesn't exclude anyone. Dao Buddhism embraces evolution and sees the progress of change and it's time to put things into history now. It's time to put the main religions into history now. They have done good for us during our evolution but so much bad comes with it and its clear none of them has what it takes to bring this world further and unite us as we need. They do worse and have taken more lives than it brought good to this world. They should not be forgotten though we should be proud of our evolution, and we should study them with a yin and yang symbol on them in the future to see the opposites in them. Religions has fallen into history before, and it shall happen again. We can't have all this different religions and views of life when they all mean the same but causes so much friction between us. They served a purpose once but are long obsolete. We must see the bigger picture now and accept that universe is part of us as well as we are part of universe. Looking at history religions has a dark shade. Hunting minorities just because they are different. Diversity is our greatest strength, and we should be proud over our differences. Just because we put our religion in history, we should not lose faith. Because faith is important, and we need it in our lives. But we put our faith in our self and our future to be and the afterlife that is so much bigger than a simple god. We must learn to be able to embrace eternity in a new way because there is no beginning and no end to this, we are just a small part of this beautiful universe and it's there to be explored by us. We must become care takers of earth and explorers of universe.

...

.

- It's up to us to make it happen not to anyone else. No one will do it for us. It starts with you and me.

We must stop living in a lie. We must see the truth as it is and live by it. We live in an old world today based on values from religions made up thousands of years ago. We must end the old and start living in the new world. It's not an end it's a new beginning. The norms of today won't exist tomorrow. Everything is already in place to make this happen. We have reached a point when it is time to take our next step. We have reached far into the information technology age and the next step isn't physical but its mentally. This is a time for everyone to make a change, a change for the better. For the old people that hasn't done much to help the earth. They have a chance to finally do something right. For the old it's the hardest but this is an opportunity they can't miss. There is no time to be selfish and feel sorry for yourself about all the changes but to be the bigger one and do it for our future. This is for our future; this is for our planet. This is the biggest step we have ever taken. This is bigger than you and me, it's about humanity taking the step into eternity into infinity. This is about us taking the final step to become a higher form of civilization. This isn't just a temporary change that will help us in the near future. It's a change for eternity even for when we have left this planet for good. This is about making our species a part of universe for ever. There is no time to feel foolish or upset over that you haven't seen the truth till now. Its evolution and this are the way things go. There will be millions of evolutionary steps if you just get a grip and make this step. Change is part of our nature, both big and small changes. Change is a natural state of nature and takes place during all of our existence,

change has existed as long as universe itself and will
always be.

...

.

- The first book might have upset
you, but it's simply the truth as
it is, and we have to move on from
the old world and shape up majorly.

.

The people of today will have a new purpose and
meaning to life. This future will expand this planet
out in space and go on forever. This is a unique time
we live in, a time where all the loose ends come
together and starts a new beginning. A time where
we really learn from our past and put thoughts into
action. We set the rules for how ours and others
civilization will evolve and what checkpoints to go
through. We will amend evolutionary thinking and
start a new era of how things will evolve. When this
happens, we will start to have control over our own
future, we will gear our own evolution in the
direction we want. We will do it by taking many steps
enough in order to reach our goal. This time it will be
a whole planet aiming for the same direction in all
areas and working together as one. It's not like we
will do the same things as everyone, but we will have
a mindset that enhances us and strive to reach the
goal. We will be able to plan every step we take in
any direction we want. There will come times when
the only option is to work as one, a situation we can't
handle with today's world. We will stand before

challenges that are out of proportion and we can overcome anything by working together and function as one unit. This is all in a distant future and we have plenty of time to reach that goal. We will start to invest time in our future evolutionary steps we take and will be able to make estimations on when the goals will be reached. The beauty of this is that we only have to take many steps enough in order to reach our goal. Then we will fulfil it and fine tune it and evolve that too. Of course, there will come new discovery's that will change the course of our path, but we won't have any problem adjusting to that. It's only a question about time.

...
.

.

This is the way we must go in order to survive the future. We must take this step, in order to be able to continue to exist. Today we consume without any ideas how our future generation will manage to live and survive. We just use up all resources and don't have our future generations in mind of how they will manage to live and continue to evolve. Today the way we live, this planets resources will deplete and vanish so our future generation will exceed to exist. We live a way of life that will end our and this planets existence prematurely. It's an unresponsible way of life and very selfish mentality we have today. We simply can't go on in this old mentality of living, we have to make drastically change in how we live in order for our future generations to stand a chance to survive. The way we live today will not only deplete our resources, but our wildlife will get extinct as well. Today massive of natural life get extinct and that's only because we are careless and reckless about how we live. We need to save our diversity in nature and keep it as great as possible for our future to continue to spire. Our diversity is the key for our future evolution, and it is in great need of first aid as it is now, the fewer species there are left the poorer our evolution will become in the future. We won't survive if we don't come together and live as one planet united working together. We must be able to manage this planet as one living organism rather than the way of life today where we more remind us of the life of a parasite. We must become predators once again and live as this planet caretaker. In the future we will caretake many planets and become caretakers of universe. The way we are living today we are killing this planet, and it goes faster and faster. Today we are closer to 8 billion people on this planet, and we will grow fast. With this amount of people, the earth as we use to know it won't live long. We can't get on with the old way of life when our ever-growing population is getting massively bigger than it used to be. With this big population we must start managing the planets resources and plan its wildlife so it will last and be enough for all of us. This is a necessary change that we simply must choose in order to continue to exist. We can't go on and live as we did when it was only 4 or 5 billion people on this planet. When we live as one planet united, we can start planning and manage life on it, so it flourishes and grow instead of shrinking and exceeds. We can plan our wildlife and look after it and make sure its regrowth's where it needs to be regrown and make sure that it always big enough for our diversity to continue to exist and to evolve. We will be able to plan the areas of provision on this planet to always be enough for our entire population. By starting to plan our resources we will manage to expand and grow as planet as long as possible. We are closing in on an age where we will be exploring space and eventually populate other planet and it's important that we treat this planet with great respect and care so that it lasts for future generations. Generations of today haven't done much for future generations and that will be a great change for people of today. We have to start embracing generational thinking and evolutionary thinking. We must leave the old world behind us and start all over again from scratch with this evolutionary step. We will have year 0 again as the new world takes place and makes all the changes in the world of today.

...

.

- People should be ashamed over the way they live today.

.

The change won't happen over a night. It will take about 5-15 years to get everything in place once many people enough have come to the mind to live in the new world and many countries enough decided to join this venture. You see the whole world doesn't need to join up for this to start to take change. Only many countries enough will do. The rest will come in time. But it is quite many countries that must gather up to be able to start the alteration. We will need to make sure we have all the basic foods and resources that we need for our population to be good to live. We will start to live in a mixed mood where we still have currency to trade with the old world and make it possible for tourists to come. Everything will be managed by quota of resources and food. We will always have enough for everyone and not just a minimum living but a good living and that is all possible with nature management. We will be able to set aside areas of land enough to make sure we all have a great living standard with enough animals and nature resources for us to live.

- But we must be smart!

We shouldn't just let a few come up with our quota system but let scientist all over the world work out the greatest system ever so that we have the very best to live with. In the future everyone competes in how to make things better for us and that's something to get used to. Because we don't have to worry about money, we only invest in the time it takes to implement the changes. One way to go is to have a plastic card with all the details for each and every one or even better use biometrical system with fingerprints or eye scanner. It's just a matter of coming up with the very best solution for the people of earth to live by. In the beginning we will start to plan and prepare for the future way of life. Start planning areas of land for food and living, making plans for basic needs such as electricity, water, and waste management. We will have two systems going in the beginning as parallel to each other, one for the new free world and one for the old world. The old-world system is only for show but a necessity for us to coexist together. We will start cleansing the world from old polluting ways and step by step make things as environmentally friendly as possible. We will start populating electric cars completely and get rid of all the old cars, making sure there is electric chargers enough all over the world or in the beginning in all the countries that's in this. We will invest a lot of time in science and how to make everything much better and always keep the environment as number one priority. We will plan our natural resources so that wildlife always has room to grow and flourish, making sure this will always be a green planet with fresh nature and great diversity. We will start to see a new planet and a new life come in place. We will start using more eco-friendly products and make waste management as healthy as possible. We will plan waste management after this planets capacity and make sure that it's not going over the edge. We will raise the bar for eco-friendly resources and keep evolving it until it's no longer a burden for our environment. We will have all these possibilities because of the new world and its financial system of time.

...

.

We will invest a lot of time in science and there will be a lot more scientists then today. Education will become a major important part of our existence, and we will make it so there is always time to educate yourself. Because evolution goes much faster since we reached the information technology age there will be need to re-educate in life to keep up with the progress of our evolution. Schools will become majorly important to us, and you should be able to educate yourself no matter how old or young you are or how you have done it earlier in life you should always have a chance to pick up where you left of or reimburse your earlier studies. Education and work will be equalized since both are equally important to our existence and ongoing evolution. Student on a higher level will play an important part in our evolutionary progress when they will be aiding scientists to reach new goals. Students and workers will stay close together with cooperation between them so that we always stay on top of things and keep evolving as good as possible. You will be able to live your life and work within one area until you feel that you are done with that and then go back to re-educate yourself and start a completely new era of your life. You never have to worry about finance but live your life after your heart all the way. Education will be a big and important part of our life. Most people will become some sort of specialist within an area of field and work deeply on evolving that area. School will always be at top and teachers will re-educate themselves many times to stay in the lead of their area of expertise. Not everyone will be specialized in an area, many will live so called normal life's and do normal work. But with this new eco system of education there will always be a little bit more to it.

...

.

.

Health care will have major improvements in their existence. Now there won't be a problem with enough staff to take care of people because of bad budget. A lot of research and investments in science around healthcare will be provided. Ensuring we always have the best possibilities there is for us to handle whatever comes up. We will have enough people to properly take care of the elderly and the handicapped. Now they will have lots of time to spend with each and every one so they can fill people's life with meaning and gratefulness. In a world without money people that want to work with people and help others can really do that and put all their efforts in without having to worry about and suffer from bad circumstances which will make them happier with their work and more satisfied. There will be a lot of progress within both science and technology to aid the ill and the wounded ones. With more investment in science their will come cures for everything eventually and we will advance incredibly much with in the science of medicine just by investing more time into that field.

...

.

There will be people that won't work and that's a fine option as well. Everyone must make the elementary to go to primary school and get a default education after that it's up to everyone to get on with their life as they feel like. However, there will be perks to continue educate yourself and work. When doing nothing but living life you get a basic quota for you to live in a normal (not too much) apartment and food enough to live on (not too little) still good enough but when you educate yourself and work you get a little bit more of everything. You will get little rewards everywhere by educating or working not just self-actualization but as perks in life that makes life more joyful. Work and education are also rewarded with great honour and the whole world is based upon bringing our species further. However, there will always be people that don't want to work or educate themselves maybe just a period in their life and that's just fine. Most people want to have something to do since its their identity and helps them feel good about them self. Then there are a few that will go thru life just living it and enjoying everything there is to be, without work or education. That's just the way we are, and we shouldn't fight it. We are all equally important and we are all equally different. The quota system will be rewarding for those who strive to make a difference and bring us further in evolution but never on the cost of the basic right to existence. We should all have the right to a good life with great quality no matter what we choose to do in life. This is only possible with time as currency, and we need to have that in place, sooner than later is better. The choice of having a work won't be that hard since we will have 6 hours shifts 4 times a day so it will be open 24 hours a day. It won't take up that much time of you and you will have plenty of free time to do whatever you feel like doing. Great for parents who will have more time with their kids and the family. 6-hour workday is only possible with time as currency it won't work in the world of money. This is necessary for us when population is doubled from today and that isn't very far in the future, we grow fast now maybe 15 to 25 years until that is true, or maybe more I'll leave that for the experts to be told. The way of today might work for a few more years but we will soon be so many people that money will ruin everything for us. We can't sustain a normal world with money soon. With the population doubled and with that many people in the future and even more people further ahead and money it's almost impossible for us to become caretaker of this planet even less the rest of universe. There won't be enough money to take care of all the needs such as waste management and healthcare and the food supply will be ruined and no care about the nature if we live in a world with money. Not to mention there will only be a few that has money enough to live a good life. We can't support equality with money not even today its even between us. Thru ought our history we constantly failed to achieve equality with financial means.

...

.

There will be people that succeed in using up the quota before it resets. For that purpose, we have a basic existence quota in place in case they still need anything. The basic existence quota is done so you only can get what you need to live fore the day and is reset each day till next week. But I doubt that it will happen since the normal quota system is generous and should last without any problem the whole week. The basic system is not a punishment but a final resort in case there ever would be a need of it. If this is repeated two weeks in a row the person will get basic existence quota for another week as well just to mark the unresponsible way of living. And if the person once again prematurely ends the quota, then the person gets basic quota for a whole month. The quota misuse resets after a month. It could happen to the best even if it is not likely. The basic existence quota will contain food for the day and the absolute must have to live a normal day. This is to teach people with extreme abuse of the system to treat it properly. Notice that it is an extreme use of the quota system since it will be hard to actually exceed the quota limit. This is all possible when we are managing the planet resources as a whole and we no longer have a problem with supply of resources. There will be resources that suffer from bad harvest due to bad weather condition for that period and resources will vary in access to how much there is. That will be controlled by adjusting the quota system, so it reflects the asset of each resource. The quota system will be alive and adjusted after the situation and availability of resources. The quota system will always be maintained with the future in mind. When we manage a planet out of our needs rather than financial interest the situation is completely different. We will have no problem with allocating new areas for supply of our needs and reallocate resources as we see needed when its necessary. Remember that we live in a time where time is currency and not money. This planet contains much enough areas for supply of food and other necessities that we need in our lives. This is not possible in a world of money. We will put heavy effort in renewable resources and make sure the cycle of nature's eco system is very healthy and at its optimal existence at all times. We will have laws that reimburse the cycle of life when we plan and use resources. We will make sure that the forests are always regrown in same or more manner than we consume. The planet now stands a fair chance to regrow and maintain its rich diversity in its natural flora. This is already done in a less successful way today and is only possible to achieve to its fullest when we live in a world with time as currency. When managing the planet as a living organism and as a foundation to our resources we will be able to maintain our self and our planet in a healthy and manageable way. When our population grow big enough this is the only way to continue to exist because then we will have to manage every resource very carefully. When our population is big enough then it is vital that we can plan and control the planets resources, so it is enough for all of us. It is also vital that we can calibrate what this planet limit is in population because the planet does have a limit. And we need to become aware of that sooner than later. This is far ahead in the future when the planet reaches its limit. And we will probably already then habitat other planets as well. Nevertheless, this kind of understanding is vital in many ways because we will need to keep this in mind for our future evolutionary progress and carefully plan how much resources we put in future evolement of growing food supplies for our population. We will evolve in how we produce food as well and we will come up with new ways of maximising the outcome of our nutrition's. With the power of "we are" we are able to live a life without any limits. We will live in a world full of opportunities and evolve in ways you can't possibly imagine today. The world's population will grow to big for the world of today to handle. And it is just a question of time when that will happen. We are just in time to start making this change. In the world today it concerns with growing much enough while in the future we will consider growing manageable enough. The world of today can't handle the future population, the world of money is a failure in continued existence. Only when the world is one world, one nation, one language, one timeline and time as financial eco system we will be able to handle what the future behold for us and continue our existence as normal. This is about our future into eternity into infinity.

...

.

- you must see the truth as it is and not as you think it is.

The planet will be considered a living organism that houses life upon it, and we will treat its resources with utterly care and respect. When everyone one has joined in, and we finally become one planet one nation. The big things will start to happen. We will start looking at the planet in a completely new perspective. We will plan all land and sea masses and there will be a lot of preparation before we finally hit defcon 0. We will live with money for a while before everything is ready to go over to the new world but it's our money, this planets money so we don't really have to live poor before it completely changes. We have to remember that we created this system with money, and we can create a system without money just as well. We must make places for all the farmers that needs to be in order to provide all the necessary food for us. We must plan out the wildlife reserves over the entire planet and prepare for regrowth where it's needed. We must collect seeds from all trees and flowers and bushes so we always can regrow and expand our nature when needed. We must calibrate the life of the sea so we can repopulate the fish and sea life that need to be reproduced. We must make sure that both farmers and fishermen take care of reproduction of its used resources. Reproduction will become an equal major focus for those who work with it. We must calibrate the static resources on this planet so that we mine and drill in proportion of what's needed and that we don't deplete it prematurely. We also need to calibrate for how long we will have those resources and when is the minimum time for us to go look for it on other planets or find a substitute for it before it's too late. We have to create enormous databases to capture all DNA and information about all our ecosystem. And we must have systems for quotas and resource balance. All this will happen when we first join forces and decide to become the new world with only partial countries and regions but in smaller scale. The real big change comes when everyone is in the new world, and we have the entire planet to our disposal. We will have to start plan the living areas for both now time and future time. We will have designated areas to build and grow as population and we will become masters at building in hight when our numbers get big enough on this planet. We will build with great imagination and fantasy making the most beautiful cities we can ever imagine. We will compete in architectural design and let the most creative and most beautiful designs be built. We will reflect our past culture in each area be shown so we always remember our roots. We will make our cities gorgeous and vibrating with culture. Amazing shapes and forms on our buildings will dazzle us wherever we go. We must take this opportunity for a fresh start and do the best of it. There will be a lot of competing between us in the future in order to get the best of the best in almost every situation. In this way we keep the stimuli of competition between each other, and we nurture our efforts to go that little extra step and preform our best. Remember everything we do we do it for us, for our future to come. We no longer need to worry about money we only need to worry about time and in the sense how long time we still have left on this planet. The end date for when we must leave and become space travellers for real. Meaning all of us. Our main concern is how much time do we have left on this beautiful planet and to become as advanced as possible before that day comes. So that we can journey through space with as rich and powerful life as possible. Our quest to explore the moon and Mars in the near future is of the greatest importance for us and our evolution in space journeys and how to exist in space. We still have loads of time before that day comes, but it might be closer than we hoped. It all depends on what this planet limit is to population growth. Because it has a limit for what it can handle. And if that's not the problem we have another limit and that's when the planet explodes into the sun but that's a very long time until that happens.

...

.

.

We must start considering us as one unity, as a massive unit. We must learn how to say, "we are" and not just "I am" as we done until now. First, we got to find our self in order to be able to say, "we are". We are one unity we all come from the same roots we are all humans with different shapes and colours. Roots do unite as the great Bob Marley said and we all are the same species and its time we stood up for us and started to see the humans as the true defender and caretaker of this planet. We must start seeing us in the bigger picture. Our evolution and what's our next natural step to take. We must see us for what we are, the species human being. We existed for 200.000 years and thru our existence we have had myths, religions and societies that has come and gone away. This is a natural step for us humans to take, to put old religions behind us. To grow as species and take responsibility for the planet that have given us so much, always giving never ask for anything back. It's time for us to start give back to the planet. It's time to protect and caretake this planet with all our heart and to give this planet a final moment of peace and make it proud over producing such a fine species as the humans. We happen to be this planet top of the chain species and there is no time for our planet to bring up another species to carry on out in space if we would wipe our self out. This planet has evolved for millions of years and had all kinds of land life and sea life and then a pixel of its existence it produces the species human being so fragile and yet so excellent. We should be proud over our planet and grateful it has been so marvellous to produce such a complex species as us humans. We all come from planet earth and that's our true roots no matter you like it or not. We must embrace how diverse we are because that's our true nature. We have reached a time where technological progress happens so fast, we are no longer reacting to change. A time when our population grows faster than ever before and will continue to do so. This is a natural step for us to take and it will happen even if not immediately but over time. It is time for us to wake up and smell the roses. To see the truth about our existence and to start taking the responsibility we are supposed to take. There is a bigger picture then just living your life and work, eat and sleep. We have passed thru so many evolutionary steps and there is endless of steps to take if we just wake up and start take responsibility. This is the evolutionary step the awakening and it is happening for real. It's time to wake up from a thousand of years of coma where we believed that diversity is dangerous and chasing false happiness for so called money where we have had a minority living the life of a lifetime and the masses working their assess of in order to make it thru. Where some people haven't even had a home to go to. Where people have been slaves for a group of people, and we have had a fake hierarchy where only a few selected ones has been treated as kings. It is time to wake up and see that our true nature is sexual, and that the old world has clouded our view of what's normal and not. Religions has hold us back and blinded us from the truth for thousands of years and it's time to put an end to it. We need to wake up and start take responsibility over our planet. The way we live today we are nothing but parasites leaching from this planet sucking it dry. We are better than that. We do have what it takes to step up and save this planet for as long as possible. And we do have what it takes to bring this species further into infinity into eternity.

...

.

- Yeah, that's what we are talking about. Bringing our species into infinity into eternity.

.

There is no end and there is no beginning, universe has existed for eternity already and we just happen to be lucky enough to be a part of it. Question is do we want to continue to be a part of it or do we just want to be a blip in its ancient. The universe contains mysteries and wisdom in its ancient and we have the humble opportunity to be a part of it and to explore it all thru generations of generations. There is billions of galaxies and the chance that we would be alone is quite slim. We will meet aliens and that day we have to be prepared. By the time we stumble upon alien life we must become advanced enough for us to outmanoeuvre them and be superior in every way. We will only accept diversity is our greatest strength and aim to coexist with them unless they declare war. Then we defend our self. We shouldn't stray away from our principle we should strive for peace with any species we stumble upon. Universe isn't ours its everyone's and we just happen to be a part of it. We are caretakers and defenders of this planet and universe, and we should never stray away from that. We raise above simple greed and hunger for destruction. We are talking about infinity into eternity here, that's a very long time. We will evolve many times over and who knows what the future holds for us. We owe this to our next coming generations. We must start seeing what kind of responsibility comes with being number one species on a planet. We can't keep sleeping and not see the truth. Our spaceships will evolve, and our massive fleet will travel great distances, and we will find new planets to populate and some we will leave alone to its own evolution. We will be journeyman of space one day and that's pretty impressive.

...

.

- Welcone dear. Into the future.

.

By living in a world without money as currency we will have eliminated the factor of greed for power completely. We will redirect the element of greed towards the progress of our evolution and knowledge. We will no longer have a few with tons of money living a life in luxury but everyone will be equally rich in life. It will be a completely new world order, and we will eliminate the gap between societies completely. This way we will have a new way of equality. We will no longer segregate different groups of people and man, and woman will be equal in all ways since salary won't be a factor anymore. It won't matter where you are born or in what family you are born but we will all have the same chance in life. And that's a great strength we are missing out today. Instead of having a small group of selected ones bringing this world forward we will have a major army of intellects that will work for our future together. We will become so much stronger and brighter with a world without money it's not even comparable with the world we live in today. We would have almost eight billion people that would educate them self as much as they want and become high scholars of different areas compared to just a margin of that that can afford a good education. We would be a top-notch planet with billions of brilliant minds working to bring us the greatest life we could ever have. It will become a completely new eco system of education that will grow vastly over time. The status of teacher will become majorly honourable and will not even be close as bad as it is today. In every corner of the world, we will have a new young brilliant mind that breaks the barrier of what can be done. We wouldn't be able to take care of all those brilliant minds in a world with money. Fact is as it is today, we can't take care of the few ones we have. But that's not the case in a world where time is currency then we can take care and nurture every single one of us because all it costs is time. When all this is in motion and the eco system starts to work at its fully function the evolutionary progress will start to go faster than before. We will have updates and patches to our existence with a few years interval. We will be a planet in constant motion and a planet that never sleeps when the population grow big enough.

...
.

.

We will still need a police force all over the world to keep everything nice and comfortable for everyone and to maintain law and order, but crimes will go down since the absent of unjust treatment of life standard is completely gone. Without money we won't have any reason to commit crime in order to gain benefits for our self. But there is still violence that needs to be dealt with but that will go down as well. We will have a completely different world to live in when we are in the new world. At first before all this happens there will be a lot of chaos. A lot of people will have a hard time accepting the truth as it is, and a lot of people will get upset with the facts coming with this. There will be a lot of wild discussions, and a lot of denial will happen. Some will go backwards and hide from the truth as good as they can. In the beginning people will be divided between accepting and non-acceptance. But the longer the time goes, more and more will wake up and see the truth. It will be a loud and noisy waking up from a long slumber. People will deny and call it lies and become horrible versions of them self. But it's necessary, this is a must for us to be able to take this step and bring our species into the future instead of getting extinct. Some people will deny it long and hard. All we can do is have a lot of patience and spread this message as good as we can. This is a new beginning; this is the beginning of the greatest step humans ever taken. This is the final step we take before we start the journey as a higher form of civilization. Over time enough people will have come to their senses so that this will be the path we take. It might take long time it might take shorter time the important thing is these starts moving and people start to wake up one by one, step by step.

...

.

.

The quota system would be based on points. The points would be based on supply and demand and the availability of the product. For food the points would be distributed in relation to supply and the amount you would get every week. Every week you get a certain number of points so you can get what you need. It will be a good number of points that will give you more than enough groceries for that week. It will be so you can choose to eat out all week or buy food home. If you have a family the points will be adjusted to that situation. The points will be adjusted so that it knows if its food or magazines or anything else you are getting, and it will be reflected on the quota. There will be a quota on everything, if its electronics it will be a quota on how many of a certain item you can have per person. It will consider of renewal circle. If renewing some item, the recycling will be considered. So, you register a return of the old product and can get a new one after that. Same goes for cars and boats and other vehicles, the quota will be on the number of items you can have per person. Healthcare will be free, just like there is business quota for resource consuming companies there will be medicine quota that doctors approve for, if needing prescription medicine to treat your illness. Movies and music will be free and phone calls and internet would be free. The companies would get company quota for their needs of resources based on availability and future plans of how to sustain the resource. This way we can manage resources all over the planet to last as long as possible. That goes for the static resources, the renewable ones will be carefully monitored that they are renewed in a manner that's satisfying. When it comes to IT software will be free and hardware will be on quota. Exactly how the quota system is going to be is left to be created by having a competition between scientists all over the world to create the most perfect quota system and the best one we choose. The points will start getting distributed at a certain age decided by all of us. Let's say the age of ten just for the sake of it. But then you won't get a full score but a little chunk so you can get some toys or whatever you need at that age. And that will remain until you get authoritative then you will get a full score and can be as any adult is. All this will be monitored and revised every month and adjustments to behavioural patterns will be made accordingly. There will be static quota points and floating quota points. The floating quota points gets reset each week so you can't save points there, for example food points. Others such as cars and house quota points will be static and last as long as you have them. There will be a party point so you can get extra enough to throw a party every now and then as well. You will always have enough to have friend over at dinner. It will be a complexed quota system that will be perfected and completed when the whole planet is onboard. But it will be up and running from day one when we are many enough to start the new world. There will be quota on traveling in different ways. Electric cars are free, trains there will be a ticket system in place to make sure there are enough seats, but it will be free from quota and airplanes have quota and boats without electric engine or sailing has quota. Basically, anything that consumes resources or is a constrain on nature will have quota. We will utilize quota to sort use of resources out.

...

.

We only need one language. We have invented way over one hundred languages and we only need one. When we enter the new world as one unity, we must do that to one hundred percent. To be more correct we only need one world language. One language that is spoken and written all over the world. We must choose a common tung for us to speak so we all can understand each other. Communication is of major importance for us in the future. We can all keep our native tung, but we need to have a second language that will be our main language so we all can communicate with each other no matter where we are. The world language should be taught already from elementary school so that everyone has it as a second mother tung. We will be bilingual by nature. And we can choose to learn more languages if it's in our interest. But it's out of utterly importance we have a world language. We are one planet, and we will have one united language. We can do this in two ways either we choose an already existing language as our new nation language, or we make a completely new one. That won't be a problem we can easily create a new language, but the hard part is to get everyone to start using it. We will let everyone have a say in this like with everything else. We simply vote for the suggested languages we have and let the top choice become our new world language. Languages are an important part of our identity it defines who we are in more than one way, it's a part of our culture and now we will have a new culture and a new identity with the new world and all what that means. The world language will be used on each nations TV on many channels and movies will be in the world language and so will also radio be. The internet will change to the new world language as well. We will make sure that the new language is influencing us majorly in any way possible so it's a natural choice for us to use it. A common language is important for us, it will unite us and make us whole as one unity. We will use all media to influence us with this language and we will be able to communicate with the entire world. Since we can move around and live wherever we want to in this world this is a must for us. Not to mention all the politics and decisions about the world will be made in this language. We will break down the language barrier and open up a completely new world which is a perfect fit with the new world order. No matter what the new language of this planet will be it will be a game changer like nothing else. And if we choose an already existing language, the ones that has it as mother tung today can choose to read a second language in school at free choice, so they too become bilingual. It will not only break down the barrier between languages but also cultures, now we can all communicate our culture and history and create a greater understanding of each other. It will take a while but eventually everyone will be able to communicate with each other and things will change majorly. We will become brothers and sisters all over the planet and we will be proud over our different cultures. It won't matter where your origins are from, we are all equally different and we can all understand each other. By breaking down barrier after barrier we will grow closer to each other, and our unity will grow so much stronger.

...

.

.

The way we live today works fine for today. We live without any mind of the consequences of tomorrow. Today we don't care about future generations and how it will be for them to live. We consume as if there is no limit to anything and don't bother to think one more step ahead. The generations of today are extremely unresponsible and careless about anything but them self. The way we live today with no plan and no thought about the future we won't last long. We live without any real vision today and everyone is jaded to take responsibility for tomorrow. We are so consumed by our self today and yet we are more connected to the world than ever. The generations of today haven't put a single effort for the future generations to come when it comes to the planet. We just use and deplete this planet of its resources thinking no further than the nose reaches. Everyone likes to talk about the nature, but no one does anything about it. It's a reckless living we live today with no responsibility taken for the future. We can't have it like this anymore, we must wake up and start take responsibility for the future to come. We must start using generational thinking for real. We can't just think well it works now so there is no problem. We can't just assume someone will take care of it or it will work out fine. We must see the truth and what our possibilities are.

- This evolutionary step isn't for you or me. It's for all our coming generations to come and our species future into infinity into eternity.

This is it. This is a chance for you to do something right with your life. To do something to be remembered of. We must stop being selfish and feeling sorry about our self and do something for not just your future but for humanity as a whole. For all coming generations and for this planet. You can't be so absorbed with yourself, its time you did something for your children and your children's children. This is the final test for humanity as we are today, this is the new beginning everyone is waiting for even if it's not what they expected. We have here a chance to set the course for humanity for the rest of the time there is, in other words into eternity into infinity.

...

.

- this is your chance to be a true hero.

There will be many similarities from the new world to today. People will be registered as working or studying or unemployed just like today in order to keep the quota right. And companies still have to declare their work outcomes in order to see they are not over employing people in relation to what they do. This new system will make it so much easier for companies to exist. If they grow in demand, they simply just employ more people and if they have new projects that are uncertain, they can still employ enough people to give it a go. People can dare to take risks now and invest time in new projects that they never been able to in the world of today. This will open up for scientists to invest time into projects that use to be too costly to even try to think about it. We will have a completely new opportunity to explore new grounds that was not possible before. Of course, the world would have a main focus in our evolving process and that being governed by the leading organs of the world. We would still have a focus on the progress of our development that has been elected by the people, so we never lose track of our self. But that's just a part of everyone. There will be plenty of opportunities for the people to take part of. It will be easier to become your own entrepreneur and for you to follow your heart. It will be easy to put your efforts into a business and to give it a real chance and see if it works. If it doesn't work, you simply close shop and move on. For some of the businesses there will be quota, for example restaurants. We can't have everyone open up restaurants because it consumes resources. There will be a limit to those businesses that consumes resources and a demand of productivity as well as successful consummation of their product. So, it isn't a waste of resources. In order to open up a resource consuming business, people have to apply for a business permit and be approved for that area of expertise. Whatever you want to work with there will be an education for it, there will be many work-based education that might be a bit shorter in its program in order for you to get a license to work within that field. Even if following your heart to you means open up a business right away its better if you have a basic education within that area. There will no longer be a problem with understaffed businesses but there will be a control of over staffed places. But it will be a generous control, so you don't have to worry too much. Education and work will be equalized because its evenly important to work as it is to have the right skillset to work. If you're an artist, you have to apply for a work permit if you paint or sculpture things. But if you're an actor or singer or an entertainer of some sort then you only must register your own company. We will encourage artists no matter genre to do their work because they are so important for us and our stimuli. Artists are such a vital part of our everyday life no matter if its music or movies or theatre or opera or just art in any form. They will be celebrated and honoured for the stimuli they give us that we need so much. Without those stimuli our imagination would become dull and our inspiration to new invention would slowly fade away. Without Artists and art there would probably be a major depression, and the world would look totally different. We need entertainment no matter what mood we are in. It helps us get through hard times and it lifts us up when we are in a good mood. It channels our anger and boosts our romance. We should strive to boost our stimuli in all directions for us to have as good life as we possibly can.

...

.

.

The new world leader will be ambassadors of planet earth. It will be two people one man and one woman, reflecting our species nature. To that there will also be a supreme board with two people from each continent or domains you may call it that are advisors to the ambassadors, also one man and one woman each. Then there will be two representatives for each country or zone you may call it, also one man and one woman. The political organ will be in the form of a yin and yang with one blue drop and one red drop and green as the boarder lines. The blue drop will represent the people that are true truth or mind, and the red drop will represent the people that are true love or heart. And the green border line represents the people that are natures guardians and mother earths protectors, mother earth that gave birth to human beings. The blue and red representatives will grow and shrink in relation to the condition of planet earth. The blue drop will concern with true truth and mind matters such as science and its progress and the red drop will concern with heartly matters such as the wellbeing of the population. The green ones will have the ultimate say in everything with mother nature as primal priority. In the new world we will vote electronically with the combination of one voting app and one identity app so there will only be one vote per person, in this way people can vote with their phones or computers or whatever device they choose to use and don't have to go to a location to participate. This will make people more involved and raise the number of participants in each vote. The political organ will be elected every eight years so there is time enough to make a decent progress for each pair of ambassadors. There is also a scientific faculty that is based all over the world whose task is to support the political organ no matter who they are. The science faculty consists of top scientist teams from all areas of expertise and are of major importance to the political organ. The science faculty will on its hand always work with each and every country's elite such as magister, doctorate and master's as well as students on universities. They will all play a vital part in the process of evolution. Each country will have an organ of a red and blue yin and yang with green boarders to look over the zones progress and maintaining its wellbeing. The leaders of those organs are the ones represented with the ambassadors. In order to be in politic, you have to educate yourself with relational thinking, generational thinking, evolutionary thinking, opposite thinking and lose ends thinking and many more topics. The red and the blue drop will take turns in being out with the people and getting to know the people as they are there and then. While the other drop calibrates the needs reported back to them. Keeping a healthy balance between mind and heart, soul and spirit. There will be parties representing blue, red and green and from them they will be voted into the organ of yin and yang in every zone. There will always be fifty/fifty of men and women in politics. This way we have local knowledge and overall knowledge about this planet.

...

.

.

There is a middle step that needs to be taken before we will have everything in place for the new world. And that is when we all joined together, we need to get one currency in money to be able to see the whole picture and get the right understanding of our completeness. Maybe I shouldn't say we need to, but we might just have to take that step. And that will be a good practice of what is to come in future progress. It will be the most short-lived currency that has ever existed. It's nothing new about that step it has been done before and isn't any problem at all. Only difference is now we don't have to meet any demands of wellbeing because that's not our goal. We just must see our common resources and even out the economy before we switch over to time as currency. This middle step currency is the one we use to trade with the old world when we have moved on to time as currency. As mentioned before, we will have two financial systems in place for a while when there is still an old world and new world coexisting together. For how long that is left in use is left to find out.

- And now it all starts.

Now we will get a taste of what it will be like in the future. When we create the new financial eco system, we will let every country compete with each other to come up with a system in order to get the best system there is for us to live with. Every country will produce a DNA strain of financial eco system for us to choose from. We will not discard any choice completely, but we will choose from them and let a few moves on to the finals. With all the existing systems we have now, we will look at them and pick out the bits that are best even from those who didn't get elected to move on. In this way we will get the absolute best system there is. We will take the bits that are good and put them together with the ones that moved on. This is how we build a road to walk on instead of just a thin line of DNA strains. We will only need to take many steps enough to be able to move on and we do it step by step one step at a time.

- When I say DNA strain it means that we are dealing with living eco system that effect our lives and therefore become biological. Just like DNA contains variables of codes that decides how you look, and work so does the eco system do for us as a planet. And also, just like DNA can be tweaked and cut out and put together in different parts so can the eco system.

The science faculty will keep an overview of how its progressing and report to the political organ who will explain it to the people with help of the science faculty. This will be represented on TV like a TV show only this is about our future to be. At first the concept will be presented, and the different zones will give us an idea of what they have in mind. then after a certain time decided by all involved the show will start for real. This time it will be the financial elite in every country that does the math and come up with a great system. When the whole world is in this venture

then each continent will select one or two
winner that represents in the final. Now we just
select 5-10 finalists because we don't know how
many countries on which continents will be in
this. First the show will present the different
ideas one at a time with each zone explaining the
purpose and consequences of their system. It
will be mixed with entertainment and
simplifications from the political organ. It will run
over 5 – 10 shows or maybe more so every zone
has a fair chance to present their idea. In each
show in the end there will be a vote for who's
going to the final. It will be done electrically just
like many shows today. The entire nation gets to
vote, and it will go on for a few days so people
can watch it again and really get into each idea.
After the 5 – 10 shows are done, and the finalists
has been taken out its time for medley. Here we
look upon the finalists and try to see their
weaknesses and then we look at all the
contributions and see if there is anything we can
use from their solution in the finalists'
contributions. Maybe there is no weakness in
any of them but there might be some real
goodies in the ones that didn't make it to the
final. This will be done by the science faculty and
the expert teams of each zone. There will be a
couple of shows of puzzling and there will be no
voting this time. Maybe they will come up with a
completely new system out of the ones that was
suggested, in that case that one will go to the

finals as well. Now it's time for the finals. The finals will show the contributions one more time both the altered and the ones that remain the same. There will be in depth explanations of each one and then there is the final vote. Again, the voting will go on for a couple of days so that everyone has a fair chance to get into the final contributions. Then it's the end game. The winner will be represented and now there is only one thing left and that is to see if the science faculty or any of the expert's team would like to alter the final contribution with any of the segments from the other contribution to get a top-notch system. If they do, they must represent the idea and explain why this would be a good idea and better than the one we already have then the people take a vote again between the new idea from the one that won. Now we finally have the ultimate system to use for us. This is just a taste of what it will be like when we use politics in the future. The show will always be hosted or co-hosted by the ambassadors. We will this way have a completely new way of building our future, we will build a road to walk on rather than a thin line and that's a major change we will benefit from.

...

.

The political organ will be more of a caretaker
and maintainer of the different systems. They
will be the ones putting the political map in place
every time there is a new progress ready. They
will deal with the final product that has been
compiled by the world elite teams. They suggest
what comes next and people vote for the
different suggestions deciding what order it will
be and see what direction we are heading. They
will be the ones that keep an eye on everything
so that it remains in control and alert if there is
something that needs a patch or an update. They
also have the vital responsibility to control the
resources of this planet and make an estimate on
how much we have both with the ones we know
of and are extracting but also the ones we still
aren't extracting. They will constantly monitor
this planets resources and update the quota
system as needed. From the progresses that are
suggested by the political organ there might be
just a few that can handle the work of it and a
major voting contest might not be possible, but
we can still vote for it to get it done in a
particular order. Some projects will be out of
bigger nature and stretch over years, then they
will give us status updates and progress reports
about that project. Some things are just a simple
matter of choice of what we want so there is just
a single vote for it, for example the world
language choice. We should probably wait with

the world language choice until seventy five percent of the world is in the new world. That's not carved in stone just a suggestion we must see what everyone feels and has to say about it. In the beginning it's a bit tricky to decide everything but we must come to an agreement all of us and then go for it, the sooner the better in my opinion.

...
.

.

We will invest in time. That means to take things slowly and be thorough in order to have as many options as possible and make the road as wide as possible when building the road of evolution. That's something that just isn't possible in today's world of money as financial eco system. Today it's all about getting things out as fast as possible and to do it as cheap as possible to make as much profit as possible. There is no thought about quality and evolvement for the future. The financial eco system of today is limiting us massively when it comes to progress in all areas just because there is not enough funding to do that. It's usually because you don't have the money to hire the needed staff that it requires. Today's worlds suffer from greed for money and power which often go hand in hand.

And it's a very destructive force that ruins a lot of opportunities and ruins a lot of lives. Today there is a huge gap between the rich and the poor and there is no sign of it getting any better, in fact it is getting worse and worse all the time. With time as currency, we will have plenty of opportunities to choose from and things will be possible beyond our wildest imagination. Money won't do it for the future of this planet it will ruin everything, and to put things straight: Time is NOT money. Time is the savour of this planet and is the only true choice to go for. When time is the financial eco system we can use as many people we need for as long time it needs in every situation and that will be a must for us in the future. Time is vital when you build roads to take many steps enough in order to reach a goal. And it can't be utilized not even near in the same extent in today's financial eco system since time and money is not even remotely close to each other. Time and money aren't really related to each other even though time is a part of money in the sense we get paid per hour. Time doesn't get its true nature revealed with the current financial eco system. To invest in time is to take the time it needs to take many steps enough to reach the goal. To invest in time means you are thoroughly in each and every step you take. The professions of today within economy will change into investors of time and will need the same amount of education as it is for economics today.

Time is a dimension of its own and shouldn't been taken lightly.

...

.

.

We are all animals of the same planet. We are all equally equipped with heart and brain. Mother nature is all about diversity, there is not one tree, flower or bush that are the same. There is not one bird, cow or bear that are the same. There is not one snowflake that are the same. There is not one single human that are the same even identical twins has differences. Why isn't that reflected in our normality norm today. The way things are today it doesn't work for the future. It's an old and outdated world we live in. It doesn't matter what colour of the skin we have or what origin we have, we are all an equal opportunity of life. The world today cannot support that fact, it's impossible for the world of today to take care of that fact. We have billions of opportunities of people today and yet there is only a fraction that get it to its full extent. It's a minority that can contribute to today's world. Where is the logic in that? It's much better if we have almost eight billion people contributing to the planet of today. We are seriously cripple our existence and evolution the way we live today.

We are losing vastly opportunities and possibilities by the way we live today where only a few are contributing to this worlds progress when we could have an army of brilliant minds that did their best to bring our planet further. We have today reached a point where our evolution is at its peak, we have started to see our planet as a whole. We have lived through world wars and matured a lot. It's time we realise we are species number one on this planet and with that comes a major responsibility. We are now in a position where we can start to take care of this planet and its future. We are in a position where we must start to take care of our self. We have come to a time when it's time for us to become a higher form of civilization, we have nothing to gain from living in a world where the majority of the planet lives in wretched poverty and misery. There is no benefit or logical reason for us to have it like this. We have reached a point when we could change all this and take care of all the areas of this planet to bring countries in poverty to an equal high standard as the rest of us. And it wouldn't be hard if all of us dug in and made it happen. Today we have the opportunity to make sure that every country can live with high standards and high education if we just wake up and see the truth. But instead, we live in a hypocrisy where we expect countries that live in poverty to raise on their own and start get educated when there is no money or resources to do that for the country where they live with civil wars and no democracy. We fail miserably to live up to the alpha race we are today. The financial eco system of today cripple us in so many ways it's outrageous. There is no longer a reason for us to have money as the financial eco system. We must wake up and unite and start building up the weakest link, always making sure we are as strong as possible as a whole. Today we are weak. We live in poverty of progress for the entire planet. Money makes us blind, blind for the true meaning of power where we all work together as one and simultaneously strive to achieve a better tomorrow. There is no problem for us to build up the infrastructure of all the countries when we leave money out of the picture. It's quite easy if you think about it. This is like lotto; do you rather play a few lines hoping to score the jackpot or do you play millions of lines in order to increase the chances to win the jackpot. Well, it's exactly the same with this planet would you rather have a few hundred thousand trying to evolve and bring this planet further or do you see almost eight billion people doing the same thing. The chance for us to come up with new solutions and making new progress increase amazingly much by living as one planet. Ok not eight billion people would do the evolving but at least a billion and that's an extreme improvement of life standards then today. It's a fact the financial eco system of money could not support that but with time as currency we can. Money is part of the problem not the solution. With money as the financial eco system the poverty will remain and grow as the population grows and it grows much faster now there is no way for this eco system to keep up. We will never achieve true equality with money as our engine. Peace is the true engine with much greater power than war. By building up the weakest link all the time by providing infrastructure and put an educational eco system in place and provide with teachers and creating responsibilities of reproduceable recourses for them and help them out in any way possible. When they are up and running, we leave them be and move on to the next weakest link and do the same thing there. We just keep doing that and by this way we are creating a never ending spiral upwards. Eventually the entire world will be a work in progress a never-ending project that will bring meaning to us all. To bring this planet further and to protect and caretake this planet for as long as possible. All this is possible if we just wake up and see the truth as it is.

...

.

- That's the true power of learning to say; We are.

In this world venture it doesn't matter how the financial status is of the country that joins it. This venture is for the future, and everyone is welcome to join it. It will only be for a while we use the new common currency of money in order to reach time as currency. We will have the money currency in use as long as the world is divided between the new world and the old world. If the country is underdeveloped, it doesn't matter because we would build that country up when times come. At first in the beginning, we would make sure the bare necessities would be in place for the country to participate in all that's happening but when time comes, and time is the financial eco system we would bring that country up to standard with all what that it means. We will always focus on the weakest link and make that stronger. Eventually we will all be equal in our existence and the weakest link will be about minor updates, now the entire world work together as one and we update the planet over and over again. It will take a while to get everyone up and running but it's not a problem because we have now taken the vital step that needs to be taken. It will be a few years of preparation when the final decision is done to create the new world. I know I said we should wait with deciding the new world language but maybe that's not possible because we need to get new educational literature made for every zone and we need to prepare our entire financial structure with a new system that can handle both money and time. We need to prepare the political system so that proper education is in place. Our first ambassadors won't be as educated as our coming ones. That doesn't mean they won't know what they are doing because they will know for sure. In the beginning it will all be new to us, and it will take a while for things to get in place. The first progress of choosing currency and financial eco system for the years to come will happen quite soon but to get it in place will take a while. And that period will be something out of a honeymoon for us to get into the new world order. We will familiarize the new political behaviour and get comfortable with how easy it will be to vote. A lot of translators will be needed in the beginning in order to reach out to all the world but that will fade in time with the new world language growing and becoming a natural way to communicate. It will be hardest for the generations of today because there will be a lot of adjustments but don't forget this evolutionary step isn't just for us, it's more for the sake of the future and the coming generations that will grow up with it as a normality. But it won't just be pain for the people of today remember we have all the recourses we need to make this happen and it will have a fast paste, lots of new education will come to hand and there will be tons of media that aids us in learning the new language if we must do that. There will be a lot of planning and research to do to manage the new planet and all its resources. It will be a busy time for sure and we will all get involved sooner or later. We don't have to worry though because we don't have to rush anything, but we should take the time needed so we get everything right and we can always adjust things that needs to be adjusted afterwards.

...

.

.

We live and exist just as much when we are retired and child, we have the same needs and feelings when we are old and young. Yet those two groups are neglected majorly, and life quality isn't good at all for them especially old people. What kind of way is that to thank them for a hard-working life providing for our planet and future? With money as financial eco system we cut down on those two groups in order to save money. What kind of world is that? As if you're not worth the same when old or young. It's like your life is worthless when you get too old. Just look at the world of money and isn't very hard to see it isn't working. When we lived our life working all the time and raised children for tomorrow done our fair share of living, then we should be treated with dignity and respect and not like some garbage that isn't worth anything. We can't take care of the old and the young with today's financial eco system of money. Same goes for healthcare we cut down on staff in order to save money what kind of thinking is that. What kind of world are we living in. Are we not supposed to be able to take care of the ill and the sick? Just stop and think for a while, have a look around you there is so much that isn't working because of the financial eco system of money it's unbelievable. In some countries the medical costs for a private person are so high they can't afford to get ill; it would ruin their life completely. Or medicine cost so much that normal people can't afford to treat their illness. Is that really the way it should be? All over the world companies make budget cuts in order to make more money, to make more profit and the first thing they cut is staff. And why do they need to make more profit it doesn't help anyone but make a few ones richer instead of having a blooming and thriving business. Money creates a bad mentality and bad progress of this world. Money was good once upon a time even if it never has been successful in creating equality it was still necessary but now it has served its purpose and are obsolete. Money has made this world unfair from the beginning of its existence. It has never been its purpose to create balance and harmony in the world.

...

.

.

We only need one law, that will cover us all. We are all the same species, and we need to strengthen our unity. We live in different worlds as it is today with different laws in each country. The way we live today we support gaps between countries and make them larger by not trying to achieve unity even though we are all the same in the base, we are all humans. Laws should reflect the truth about humans and support its possibilities. We need laws that untie and strengthen us instead of breaking us up. We can't have different laws for different group of people. We are all the same and we are sexual by nature, we need to have laws that represent the true human nature and have the same law for all of us. We need to strengthen our unity, and it should be reflected thru all our society. The law should be alive and pulsating and always reflect where we are in our evolution, The law could differ a little from continent to continent in order for us to have a varying landscape but no big differences, so we don't lose contact with each other. The law should serve our evolution as purpose and should always be in favour for us to move forward. We need strict nature laws making sure we preserve and maintain Nature and always make it flourish and bloom. The laws should be for maintaining the great diversity in Nature and always be in favour of different ways of maintaining Nature as diverse as possible. The foundation of the law should protect the diverse nature in our existence as it is and always be in favour of life itself. The law should be very strict on pollution there should be no tolerance for pollution whatsoever. The situation has changed now, we live in a world with no money, and we can put our resources in keeping the world free from pollution. We can invest in electricity in a completely new way and make a pollution free world a priority. It's an investment that will cost time and its only in the beginning it will be a lot of investment in it, in time everything will already be pollution free, and the environment will be healthier than ever. This world we are talking about now will have the chance to make the world survive humanity and flourish with us in it. This new world is a complete game changer and will give us possibility's we will never have in the world of today. The law will reflect our true devotion to our nature and mother earth. We will become true caretakers of mother earth. The law will be thoroughly defined for the quota system in place making sure it always is up to date and in balance with the current situation, making sure we always have good balance in our resources and environment. The law should protect our existence as a whole, not just us humans but also the nature we require and this planet. And it won't stop there we will have laws for how to manage other planets and how we utilise them for our coexistence and future evolution. The law will expand as we reach further and further out in space. Crime will go down in the new world because there is enough for everyone and there won't be any unjust factors in our existential existence. There will be more than enough for us all and we can start focusing on more important things in our lives and our progress. The laws are still necessary for us in order to keep everything in place and to guide and aid us in our ever moving forward evolution.

...

.

.

We must explore and learn everything there is about DNA and organism structure. Not just humans but all nature. We will learn everything there is about our internal defence system and our immune system. We will develop new cures that can cure whatever the future throw upon us.

- It's time to see the real truth about our self.

It's time we wake up and see the truth about our evolution. To start take the real responsibility we actually have. We are our own creators; we have created our self from the beginning of our existence. No one has helped us out, no god no alien. We are responsible for our own existence and everything it brings with it. We have lived of this planet as if it has no limit, we know that that's not the truth. We can't continue living like we do today if this planet shall have a chance to survive with us on it. Today we are destroying and using up nature in an ever faster growing paste. Animals are going extinct, and we do nothing about it. We just let nature die and our flora of animal is growing thinner in a faster and faster tempo every day. There are attempts to regrow nature in some parts of the world but that's not even close to enough for our nature to survive when the larger part of the world just simply doesn't care about it. some vague attempts to protect animals near extinction but that too is not enough. Thousands, and thousands of animals has gone extinct, and we just let it happen. We don't take any responsibility over animal life or nature whatsoever. Our oceans are so polluted that water life gone dead completely in big areas, and we just let it happen. The way we live today will lead to our complete extinction with this planet depleted and ruined completely with no life left to live on it. We must make a choice here. The way our population is growing we won't be able to handle life the way we have done for several thousands of years. Our fast-growing population will lead to less and less jobs and a harsher nature consumption. In order for us to exist with 15, 20 and even more billions of people we must make a choice here.

- The choice we have to make is to choose to continue to exist. Not just today and tomorrow but for eternity into infinity.

We must take a final stand, and we must make a major change in our existence today, and this is the way to do it. This is the way to choose to exist together with this planet for as long as possible, long enough for us to take many steps enough for us to become journey men of space with all life and nature from this planet preserved with us. We have to create a bigger purpose for us so that we can aim and plan what steps to take and to know why we are doing it, not like it is today when we aim aimlessly and have no idea where we are heading. We must create visions of greater existence and advanced living. So, we all know what to do next and why we are doing things in the first place. By knowing why and where we are heading more people will see the big picture and everyone will be able to do their part of the journey. We will from time to time all work as one doing everything, we can for us to take many steps enough in order to reach our next step in our evolution. This is only possible in the new world. By having a bigger goal in a bigger picture. We will unite everyone, and our coexistence will be founded on our true roots, we are all humans from planet earth. We will have great visions of our existence, and we will maintain goals bigger than just our near future. We will aim to exist for eternity into infinity and that's a very long time. By having these great goals, we will create reason for our everyday behaviours and our mentality will be reflected in the way we vision our self as creatures. We will no longer be destructive in our foundation but care a great responsibility with our everyday life. We will inspire to progress and unity, to a greater life where we all are truly equal. It's time to put today's religions into history and all unite under a common understanding. The religion is a great step in human evolution but in the long run they cause more damage than do good and are reason for our fragmented existence as it is today with so many minorities created by religions. Religions hold us back in our evolutionary progress and they are narrow-minded and prevent us from continue our evolution progress in the future. Basically, they are just filling out answers to questions we don't really have answers to. They both explain how we all come to exist and a greater power that we will get in touch with when we die. They are both the same just different versions. They have played their part and should be passed on to mythology. We should always remember them and keep the good parts from them, but we don't need blind faith in a god that does not exist. We are our own gods, and we need to start take the responsibility of that and take control of our future. Religion has created more hate and war among our self's than any other factor of our existence has. It's not good for our future, we need to stop feeling sorry for our self's and step up and make this difference happen. This is not for our self we are making this choice, it's for human mankind and mother earths existence in eternity into infinity. It's so much greater than a religion from the old world. The choice is for our kids and their kids and so on for eternity into infinity. You have a chance to be greater than anybody else ever has been. This is the greatest step in this planet's existence. We stand before a choice and the choice is to continue to exist or not. If not, everything will have been in vain. Everything will be meaningless and even the religions would have been for nothing. It's a very selfish way we live today where we think about nothing else but our self. We don't have generational thinking in our system whatsoever. We don't care about our children or their children. We only see as far as our nose reaches. We will end this planet the way we live today and that's a fact, and no one cares about it. We live so unresponsible life's today it's really scary. This planet will grow in population beyond 15 and 20 billion people, and we can't handle that the way we live today or the way the world picture is today, its doomed to fail miserably. In order to handle the complicated problems that the future holds before us the world has no other choice but to unite and work together as one. In order to not deplete this planet on all its resources prematurely we need to have a united and controlled way of using renewable resources in a matter that gives us space to evolve. When we are 20+ billion people we need to manage the planet as a whole. We can't have it like it is today where people around the world just consumes with no thought about tomorrow. When we are one planet and one nation, we can manage everything in a completely new way. We can make sure 60% of the planet is natural wildlife all the time and 20% is set aside for production of food in all its flavours. And 10% for extracting resources of all kinds with focus on renewable resources. And the last 10% is for us to expand and grow in size of population. The numbers are just an example and should always be adjusted to our population and this planet wellbeing. It should always be enough food for us to have more than enough for each and every one at all times. By managing earth this way, we will be able to handle the problems of tomorrow and we will have a healthy planet that will last much longer than it will today. The planet will survive with us on it. By managing planets, we will become not just this planet caretaker but universe caretakers. We will make sure nature has its natural causes on both planets and in universe itself. But this planet has its limits, and static resources will eventually deplete. The more we grow in population the tighter we will have to manage static resources. Our job is to make sure the static resources last long enough for us to take the next step in evolution. We must start mining static resources on other planets so that this planet resources are left as untouched as possible. Some dead planets will be purely for mining resources and others for us to start new colonies and populate them in order to bring life further. We have a time frame here. A time frame that decides we must evolve much enough to be able to start journey in space seriously and have advanced technology enough for us to make us great at it. The time frame is when we reach a stage where this planet can't hold more population as well as the availability of static resources. We must make this choice soon in order for us to stand a chance to this challenge. The selfish way we have been living for thousands of years has come to an end and its time we learn to say "We are" for real.

...

.

.

We must learn and explore everything that has to do with our planets eco system and all about its diversity that is empowering this planet. We must gather all DNA from nature and learn and understand everything there is to it. We must know everything about natures DNA and how to use it in order to be able to maintain nature and to bring it further. We will help out nature to maintain its diversity and repopulate the species that are close to extinction. We will keep banks of DNA from all species and nature vegetation so that we can reproduce it if any gets near extinction. And also research it to know what vegetation works best in what conditions and help relocating vegetation when climate is changing in areas so that we always have the best conditions for our vegetation. We will also need to understand which vegetation is best suited for different atmospheres on other planets so that we create the best possibilities to create new life on those planets. We will also learn how to create completely new vegetation and explore and learn what attributes we can benefit from. This is necessary for us in the future when we start populating other planets in order to adjust vegetation to the new conditions of that specific planet's atmosphere. We will become creators and maintainers of life and it's all a natural step in our evolution. By doing this we will expand our flora of natural resources, and we will find new substances that will aid us in both medical and other fields. We will create huge databases where all the data about DNA is stored and used for research and progress of our never-ending evolution. Whenever we reach a new system with new planets, we will collect all the information there is about it and all DNA in order to explore and learn about the newfound conditions we stumbled upon. We have the entire universe to explore and discover and we haven't even started it yet. Our existence will have so much to discover it's hard to put words on it. Universe is infinite and never ending, it is so huge it's enough for humanity for eternity into infinity to explore and discover. Our existence here on this planet will just be a blip in our timeline when we make the choice to exist in eternity into infinity. The different faiths and bad mentalities we had up till today will seem ridiculous in comparison to what we have achieved in the future. We are just children in the eye of existence timeline, and we have not even started to live as the superior species we actually are. Because we are the superior species on this planet and with that comes a major responsibility towards all life on this planet. A role we must step up and grow into and that's fast. Today we lose thousands of species that goes extinct so far and we don't do anything about it. It's so incredibly unresponsible of us to act that way, we lost massive amount of diversity and opportunities in our existence because of that. Our diverse flora is shrinking and that's fast. We can't have it like that anymore. We can't afford to lose more species. We need everything we can get for our future to come. Any species can contain the key to solve a future dilemma that we run into, we can't afford to lose any more precious life form with its unique DNA patterns and biology that could help us out in the future. We have to maintain as diverse flora as possible because every little life form counts no matter how small or insignificant it might seem today. Every life form plays its own role in this amazing wheel of life. You never know what the future will reveal for us and that's the exciting part of it all. We have no idea of how advance we will become. We only know it's all there for us to discover.

...

.

Biological technology will be a growing factor for us. We will learn how to utilize biology for technical enhancements and for any kind of technological area. Our biological tissue is far more advanced than any static matter we use in technology today. We will advance from simple things to more advanced robots that will aid us in everyday matters. And then we will be able to produce biological limbs that will replace the prosthetic we have today. We will have a new developing branch that will program biological means and advanced DNA programming. We must learn everything about the signal system in our biological bodies so we can interact and aid when needed. Biological programming is about understanding the nerve system and the different organs that are inside us. To be able to interact with the nerves signal system and to be able to communicate with the nerves and the brain. We will grow organs for donation to people that need a transplant. The way organ donation works to is absurd, it's a lottery if someone gets an organ or not and when its vital its more often not possible to get an organ. The right person must die in order for us to get an organ the way it is today. Its horrendous the way it is today. Today there is a long waiting list for people to get their organ, they are waiting for the right one to die or someone else that is the right match sacrificing their healthy body's organ to them at a high price. We can't have it like that its obscure, we will create banks with organs off all different blood types so everyone can get their organ when they really need it. We will grow organs from DNA and make sure there is always enough to everyone. No one should have to win the lottery in order to get a transplant done with the correct organ. We can't let old narrow-minded mentalities stand in our way for progression. We must be able to help everyone not just humans but animals and nature too. The organ transplant system we have today is cruel, unjust and simply horrific the way it works now. The system is outdated and malfunctioning, many people die just because we have a system that does not work as it should. We must make way for the new world and let us take control over our own future. We will have biological limbs for people who lost a hand or had to amputate a leg. We will move the medical field into the future where we no longer restrain our self from evolving and make progress in any area. We are our own true creators, and we are our own gods.

- as I said before.

We have created our self since the beginning of our existence. We have created something out of nothing over and over again we are our own reason to all the technology and science we have today. We must respect that we are our own gods and take responsibility thereafter. We must let go of old narrow-minded structure and embrace our true purpose and our true nature. We have to explore everything, the brain is an amazing processor, it executes billions of processes at the same time and can store more information than any physical device can today. We have to learn everything there is about the brain and its magical functions. Not only humans but animals too. We will come to a point where we have biological computers that can handle massive number of processes and information at the same time. We must master the programming language that brains code in so we can operate with them in far greater calibrations. In the future we will be able to connect to a master database and download whatever knowledge we need to know into our brains. We will raise our awareness to new hights. We will be able to cure conditions just by inserting brain code into the brain. Education will be done by programs synced to your brain. We can learn all the languages we want just by adjusting the brain. We will focus more on the practical and become really good in everything we do. This might sound scarry to you but it's not. Everything will happen by nature if we make the choice to continue to exist. But don't worry it won't happen all at once. We do this one step at a time, so we always take many steps enough in order for us to reach the next step in our evolution. Some will happen not too far away in time while other things are way ahead into the future.

- Now, if and when this will happen there is only one answer to.

It's up to us to make that decision. We must make the choice to continue to exist in eternity into infinity.

...

.

.

Everything you have ever seen on the movie screen or read in a book about the future with all kinds of evolutionary progress is there for us to discover. Teleportation, invisibility, immortality, psychic powers, or you name it, it's all there in our future evolution and it's all there to discover. There is so much more than that, our imagination will define what paths we take and what we will reveal in the future. This is how we have created our self for thousands of years by our ability to imagine things to reach for. It's only a question about time. Time is the only true currency we can have. We have the possibility to have the most amazing future you could ever imagine by choosing to exist in eternity into infinity. Today's values mean nothing in comparison to what we will have in the future.

Everything is there for us to discover, there is no such thing as impossible. What's not possible today is tomorrow's everyday life. The future beholds so many amazing wonders and opportunities that today's world picture seems pretty dull and malfunctioning, it's not really a hard choice to make. We have eternity into infinity to exist and all the wonders that we will discover, it's not really a big deal the change we have to go thru now. But we still must make the choice and make it happen because the world of today will miss it out and will perish. Now, you won't live to see all that, but you will part of the most important step we take in human history. This is not the time to let old narrowminded mentalities and old religious views say what's correct and what's incorrect, it's time to be the bigger person that takes a responsible decision and makes this happen. This is for our future, for our generations to come. Life will become much better for you, and you will still experience some pretty cool stuff but that's not the important part.

...
.

.

Politicians will utilise Opposite Thinking, a methodology that is used to create a road for you to walk in order to reach a goal. You use three upside-down trees where the first tree is where you are today with all the different possibilities you have now and what you already know, and the third tree is your goal where you want to go. With the definition of the final destination and what little you know it must contain. And the second tree is the road there, that you will calibrate the road, and it will be filled out with all the discoveries and show what twist and turns you need to make and will be filled in as you make progress towards the final destination. This is a good way to keep track of progress and to map out all the discoveries you make during the journey. You might stumble upon things that might be needed to solve other progresses in other goals. The purpose with this methodology is to get a good overview and to be able to plan strategies for how to proceed and to see what possibilities comes next. To know what you must do in order to succeed in reaching the goal and to know why you are doing certain steps, so you have greater motivation doing it.

Politician will also utilize Generational Thinking; it concerns the today existing different generation living on the planet. Making sure we all have a good living no matter what generation we belong too. It also concerns the upcoming generations in the future and a careful planning of resources and nature so that our future is secured and safe in its existence. It's how we will coexist today with our future generation in concern at All-time. We should always calibrate the nature so that it will last for eternity into infinity. We will always have a responsibility towards the future to come and we will always make sure that we keep several generations ahead in our calibrations so that we always have plenty of time to adjust and do necessary changes. When our population reaches higher number such as 15 or 20 billion and more it will be out of major importance that we have Generational Thinking.

Lose End Thinking is needed when you path in Opposite Thinking. Especially when you get deep into progress. It's all about making sure you don't have any lose ends in your research and that all ends are followed up so you know if it was the end or discover that it continues leading to other options that might be vital for the progress to continue. We need to know everything about everything and leave nothing to the chance.

Directional Thinking is also utilized when pathing Opposite Thinking. It is a way to see what direction you need to take in order to progress further and to see what directions are left to research in order to complete the pattern of the path. It will be about twist and turns you might not recognize at first, but you will see when putting this kind of methodology at use.

Reflective Thinking is when you think about what you been researching or doing and what consequences it has on the progress. It's about gathering a picture about what has happened and see the conclusion of its outcomes. You reflect over the current situation that has been. Preflective Thinking is when before you act, you start creating a picture of what you will go through and try to prepare yourself for what is to come. Flective Thinking is when you are in the moment right now, being aware of everything you do in the very moment it happens.

Evolutionary Thinking is when you plan the future evolutionary paths to take and try to decide what comes first. Even though that might be hard since it all depends on what you discover and in what order it happens. It is also the creational process of imagine new possibilities for us to have in the future and is a vital part of our existence. We should always stimulate our imagination so that we keep having great visions for us to follow. It's about keeping a good overview of current evolutionary progress and making sure we are all on the right track to continue to evolve. It's about planning the order of the updates to the world and the implementation of the updates. (Update is the same as evolutionary progress achievement)

Relational Thinking is about exploring and knowing about all the relation there is here on earth but also in universe and in Metaverse. There are relations everywhere and they are constantly changing. It's about learning about your inner force and the calibration lifestyle. You harmonise with the relations in nature and your surroundings and in yourself. You learn about relations everywhere and you see the dependences of various matter and how the play together. You imbibe the atmosphere and become a part of all the relations. When you become more advanced you reach the state of being one with the relations in your surroundings.

All these schools you can become more advanced and go deeper into the different areas I just explained the foundation of them here. There are more schools as well but that I save for another time.

...

.

.

We will have big fleets of spaceships; in the beginning we will make larger spaceships that can contain more cargo. We will eventually build big space stations in space to have as platform for longer journeys and work more constant in space with crew there all the time. When we have gotten to build factories and mining facilities on the moon and on mars, we will start building larger spaceships there that has easier to lift of the planet due to gravitation. Eventually we will have larger ships that can handle heavier gravitation. And then we will have fast traveling and really large-scale ships so-called space cruisers, that we will use to journey out in space. We will become real space explorers and have large amount of population living their life in space. Our research in space technology will grow with time and become a big part of our everyday life. First, we will just explore our solar system and expand on the planets here. We will wait with deep space journey till we have evolved spacecrafts to be fast enough and big enough for us to journey over generations of people living on one and the same ship. Eventually we will have so fast spaceships that journeying in space will be a breeze compared to early days. When we are experienced space journey men, we will start exploring our nearest solar system and start utilising the planets there. We will send out small groups of reconnaissance spacecrafts that will check out unknown areas and scout out routs for us to travel, we will also send out massive fleets that will have the necessary means to start populating and rebuild our civilization on other planets. We will put in system that we have an upgrade-squad that will if we evolve much enough travel to the locations we have occupied and carry out the update there as well. It will be a hard task to keep everyone up to date, but we will grow with the task and work out systems for it. The larger area we populate the more effort it will take to keep everyone updated. But at the same time as we expand, we will also advance in progress so it will go hand in hand. We will develop large planetary scanners that will scan planets and see what kind of raw material, resources and minerals exist on that planet. We will utilize Terraforming in a much greater form then we do today. Terraforming will play a vital part for this planet when we grow in population in big numbers. When the population reaches big enough numbers, terraforming will be out of major importance to us so we can manage this planet after our needs without depleting it on its resources. Terraforming will also play an important role for us when we want to populate new planets. We will shape and form the planet as good as possible after our needs for a great start for us, but we will have to be careful, so we don't put the planets natural eco system out of balance. We will become masters of Nature and all that comes with that, we will be able to reproduce all aspects of nature eventually and make sure we always have Nature enough to provide a new eco system to other planets that lacks it. That's one big reason why it is so important we don't destroy our nature today anymore, that we stop making animals extinct and start to take serious responsibility over our planet. We need everything we can get for our future. We need as diverse flora as we can get for our future to come. That's why we need to understand and know everything there is about our nature in every direction possible, so we know how to recreate the nature we have here today. We must see the larger picture of our self and have greater visions of tomorrow, so we understand why we must do things and why it so important we do them. We are this planets caretaker, and we must shoulder that role sooner than later. When we stumble upon a planet with life already upon it, we don't force our nature to it, but we do the same thing as we did with ours, we explore and learn everything there is about it and see what new discoveries we get from that and expand our own flora with this newfound life. Nature is our new God, and its resources should be carefully used and interacted with. The richer our flora of nature is the richer our life will become, and the more opportunities we will have in the future when we explore universe. We don't know what part of our flora is best suited for different environments we will stumble upon in the future. We will need to tweak and turn on our nature so that it can suit different environments, and we don't know which part of our nature we need to use in order to get the solution for that specific environment, all our nature is out of major importance to us, and we need to have as broad flora as possible for our future to come. We can't afford to lose anymore nature, the poorer our flora is the worse it will be and the less our possibilities will be to make it in the future. We have no idea what we need to find out or what we will need to create in the future in order for us to make it to the next step, and we must make sure we have as many options as possible so that we always can take many steps enough for us to reach the next step in our evolution. By making the choice to exist in eternity into infinity we will set the bar high, we will have a must-have goal for us. By doing that we will create visions of our future to be greater and better than the ones we have today. The visions aid us to understand why we need to do things and why we must maintain nature. It gives us reason and meaning to come together as one and to take the next step in our evolution.

...

.

.

Eventually there will come a day when we stumble upon another lifeform, as long as they are not more advanced, we will have nothing to worry about and we will leave them to their own evolution so they too can evolve and take this step to become caretakers of their own planet and their evolutional progress. If they however are advanced and space journey men like us but not peaceful, we must be prepared. We must always have an advanced military even though we live in peace. We are defense only; we don't attack other civilizations. But our defense must always be top notch. We should always put focus on our military evolvement and always make progress within the military field. In the beginning we need military defense from other hostile countries that can't accept the truth and want to do us harm. There might become some war but that I don't know and is left to be found out. We will always defend our self and our vision. Our purpose is to exist in eternity into infinity and that's not possible without defense. We should always invest time in research of military technology. When the world is united as one, we will still need the military for more advanced projects and dangerous tasks out in space. Here on earth, they will help out with rebuilding the new world. The military will keep doing advanced military exercises and train in war situation as if it still was possible to happen. They should always be prepared on that something could happen. Our military should always be top notch, and the very best soldier there ever is. We need military technology for more purposes than the military. We will discover a lot of new areas that will aid us in other areas as well and that we would not find without the military focus. When we stumble upon other intelligent life form, that are hostile we will defend our self and its vital that our technology and progress is better than theirs. So, we can fight down the war fast and reach a peace between us. We will not tolerate any other mentality then caretakers of home planet and universe. And we will make that clear to anyone we stumble upon. Dao Buddhism is baseplate here on earth but also in universe. Our goal is to unite and become an equally different part of each other's existence. To coexist and harmonize with each other and learn everything there is about each other so we can all be a unified coexistence. Universe belongs to no one we are all an equal part of universe as well as universe is part of us. Universe is for the more advanced life forms that lives in harmony and that has discovered that peace is a far better engine then war is for any species. We are not alone in universe, universe is so big it goes on forever in eternity into infinity, we have no idea how many big bangs that has taken place in universe, if it is big bangs that creates a part of universe. The chances that we are alone are quite slim.

...

.

.

We will always take the role as the bigger person. We will always aid the weaker ones. Peace is a far better engine than war when it comes to evolutionary progress. It's much better to have 10 billion people working together rather than to have a few destroying each other racing in who can be the worst in destruction. It's a very destructive behavior and costs a lot of time and resources to rebuild what has been destroyed in-between wars. It belongs to the past and is no longer a valid option. War is for the weak- and narrow-minded person. When we are united and live in the new world, we will have higher education for all of us meaning there will be more people that will contribute to our progress with their knowledge. Rather than to have a few that contributes to our evolutionary progress, we will have billions of people working together to achieve advancement in our evolutionary progress. We will have so much more options and possibilities than we have today. We will become more than a thousand time stronger and advanced by living as a unified mass working together to reach advancement in our progress. The way we live today is old and jaded. It is self-destructive and it slows the progress massively in comparison to the new world and its coexistence. By having peace and unity we will have the chance to coordinate this planets resources so it will always match the size of the population, something that is not possible in the world of today when the population gets big enough. We will benefit from having billions of minds exploring and researching new possibilities rather than a few millions as it is today. We will raise as a civilization and become superior in our existence. The world of today will look like a joke to us compared to the way we will live then. This is the final test for us as human species. This is the final step for us to take before we will live in a free world in peace with each other. This is the step that will make us the superior species that we truly are, shouldering the role of being caretakers of life and peace. This is the step that finalizes our journey as a primitive species and raise to a higher form of civilization. We will all live our own life doing different things, it's not like we will be strained to only think one way, on the contrary we will fuel our diversity and always amend our individuality, but we will have a common foundation and a common vision that will unite us all. Our life standards will be so much greater then today and the further we get into the future the better it will be for us. When we live with a quota system, we will have better possibilities to build more buildings with homes and we will have no problem with electricity since we will during the startup face make sure our world has enough production for the entire world by expanding our energy production, so we always have enough. We will invest much more resources in the beginning in order to have all the needed infrastructure in place. It will be a time of rebuilding the world to fit our future to come. Instead of lacking founds to do what's needed we will give grace and let all of us do what's needed in order to have everything in place for the new world to start. We will invest a lot of time and resources into energy production and its different possibilities. We need to be able to grow with our energy since we are moving away from fossil fuels to electricity. We will utilize nuclear power as much as needed but we will invest a lot in solar, wind and water energy. We must balance the different energy resources so we can care about the planet as much as possible. We will put heavy focus on research in energy so that we can grow with the growing population. In the beginning it will be preparation and planning for the new world to come so that everything is place for the new world order. It will take some time to get everything in place and to adjust to the new way of living but it's not a problem to achieve that goal. When we do the preparation, we will still live in a world of money, but it will be our money so we can make sure everything is doable by adjusting prices and economy. The future will be about maintaining natural resources and planning after their limits. We will have a grace period with our economy during the buildup face. Most is already in place and there will be small and big adjustments in different areas. The different adjustments will all depend on which countries that will join this venture in the beginning. We won't do this change until many countries enough is onboard with it. We need to make sure we are self-sufficient in all areas of existence before we can go ahead and enter the new world. This is a process that will take time and when this will actually happen is hard to tell, maybe in a few years or 50 years or 100 years or maybe longer, only thing I know for sure is that we must make this choice in order to exist in eternity into infinity. This is the natural step for us to take now. That's where we are in our evolution and the beginning of a new era. Everything is already in place, and the adjustments needed are only so that we are sufficient for us to have as great life standard as possible. There is no reason to do this if we won't have a good life enough. We need to be thorough when calibrating our minimum needs in order to start this progress. Patience will be our friend, and we will let it take the time it needs in order to start this progress. The adjustment in our life's may look big now but when you look in the whole picture and from the future it's no big deal at all.

- That's easy for me to say hehe. Truth is...

The change will be completely mind blowing for some people and will turn their life upside down the way they live today. It's all about how conservative they are. Many will struggle with Dao Buddhism as the new normality norm but that's because we are going thru a change that is similar to when earth once was flat. This is totally necessary for us to come together as one and to have the same baseplate with the truth as it is and not as you think it is. In fact, this new world picture will improve your life quality a lot just the way it is without any external changes to the world.

...

.

.

- To explain how things will be done in the new world, I'll share this:

One planet, one nation, one currency, one timeline, one law and one language. Don't forget that. It will happen sooner or later, and we happen to live in the time era when it's about to happen. No matter when it happens the very same issues will remain. The new systems need to be developed and investigated truly. The elections will be worldwide we will all have to learn the new language we will all have to adjust our currency so that we all have the same. Our Economy system needs to be redefined in order for it to work properly. And while we are on those steps we might as well let all nations universities cooperate and compete in developing as smart financially system we can get, given the base variable Opportunity of life to use as baseline for it. We are all familiar with the concept of TV shows like "So you think you can dance" and "Idol". So, we can easily make those contest seasonal TV shows with mixed entertainment and progress shows, where all the people can call and vote for suggestions and then when each country has chosen their best solution that they will send to final that will go the year after its done, all country's presents their solution. Very much like the "Eurovision Song Contest". Only this is about our own planet's directions in our lives. In this type of communication, the first season or year depending on what we all agree upon we will have created over 195 different solutions of Eco systems of Finance, and in opposite to weakest link choice of a primal solution to erase that bit we chose the more sophisticated way and improves that area if there is a chance that is.

We will then during the entire season combine and work out solutions containing the most necessary variables that we expect out of this kind of solution, and we don't quit until we all have contributed with a complete ecosystem for finance. Utilizing every university and professor and expertise in relation to the specific Eco System. Same goes for suggestion and creation of the Eco system of language. The result is that all of a sudden we will have about 200 choices and from those 200 suggestions we will be able to choose and rebuild them into 10 superior solutions over the next season/year depending on what reality is like, These 10 Superior Ecosystems will then be the new base for what is to become our most possible advanced civilization that has ever existed within one single Ultimate Eco system of finance, one Ultimate Eco system of Communication, One Ultimate, Awesome, Erotic, Wonderful, High Tech, Existence as Protectors and care takers of life. The contest will have rules that states that to be a Valid proposal it must contain a step-by-step guide in how to move from the point we are at today, What the goal is and what the steps are to take in order to get there. It must contain a valid time estimation on how long time the different steps might take. It must also contain the need in employment sources as well as an estimation and a perfectly well-planned financial plan in that includes the following corner stone's: Costs and possibilities in resources, as in hardware, software and Employment. This must also be in relation to the Base "Opportunity of Life" and our evolutionary timeline. The Goal and God must always be the very foundation of our existence. For the Opportunity of life with us in it. To see this planet as a part of our basic needs in continuance of existence. Some of the times it won't be possible to have each nation come with solutions because the topic is too specific in requirements that only a few countries can contribute. And sometimes it's just a simple choice we have to make. The situation will vary but the main concept is there.

...

.

.

In a near future, we have to solve the sweet water situation, we have to come up with ways to produce it so there is enough for our crowded population. Today there is enough but already now there is lack or water supply in dry periods in different parts of the world in different areas of each country. Now we can solve that problem but when we grow big enough in population there will be more serious problem for us. We must come up with different solutions to produce water for us to use. And that in very large quantities. Our solutions here on earth will aid us on new planets as well, and there we will develop it even further and then take in use here on earth and so on. It's a spiral of development that we will experience in the future. When we have populated other planets there will be several civilizations that contributes to our evolutionary progress, and we will focus on different areas on different planets off course we will have our domestic areas to focus on, but we will also have a shared agenda where we coordinate our area of expertise and what we shall focus on. The more we expand the more advanced we will become. The true power of one unity will not show its true power until we have expanded much enough. The more we become the greater the combined power will be. In the beginning we will notice big changes in progress but it's nothing compared to what the future beholds for us. But in the future our evolutionary steps will take longer and longer times and require more and more out of us so it will be needed that we have one unity. One unity does not only fill its purpose in the today's world, but it does so throughout eternity into infinity. When we meet other civilizations, we will unite with them as well and share our knowledge with each other and coexist even if we keep to our own parts of universe, we are no stranger to each other. We will still allow other species to follow their own natural evolution and not interfere with each other's directional progress. We will represent mutual respect and have a humble approach towards alien species. Providing they are peaceful minded.

...

.

.

We will create other animal life forms and also update our self's. But there is no need for us to create another alpha race. We are the alpha race on this planet and that will do for a very long time. The reason I say it will do for a very long time is that we can't exclude that at some point we reach a point where we have no other choice but to create an alpha race. But that will be very far in the future and won't be necessary for a very long time. We don't know what the future holds before us and therefore we can't exclude any options. We must shoulder a major responsibility and see beyond what we understand today. We can't keep denying who we are and what our purpose is. We must shoulder our natural role of being the alpha race on this planet and start taking the responsibilities we have for real. We have to learn everything there is about all animals that exist as well as non-existent animals. There is infinite number of combinations that can exist, and we must learn about them all. We are caretakers and maintainers of nature and must know how to reproduce all of the animals there is. We will stumble upon situations where we need to invent and create the animal from scratch in order for the animal to fit the new environment or in order for us to be able to harvest something that's vital for our existence. Animals that can be a life changer for either nature itself or us as human species. Some environments will be so harsh it requires us to create a completely new flora of life both nature and animals for the planet to flourish. But it's not only animals we need to know everything about we have to know everything about our insects and bugs with all the functionally they have and what roles they play for nature to continue to exist. We can't neglect anything on this planet for our future to be. There will be a time when we have so advanced plants, they will live a life like us and be able to communicate just like we do. There is no end to possibilities, and we will have to explore them all. We must capture the natural reproduction of all nature so we can reproduce them in as many ways as possible. As I said before we will never know what the future holds before us and there is no end to the possible scenarios that we will stand before in our evolutionary progress. We also have no idea what universe holds before us in the future and what kind of evolutionary progress we need to have accomplish in order to move forward and continue explore its never-ending space.

...

.

.

The value of having a world with a united vision is massive. It's important to understand why that is. Since the beginning of our time, we have created our self from our visions and dreams. Our dreams are what makes us take another step in our evolution. Because of our visions we are able to create or invent the necessary things for us to take the next step. Because of our visions and dreams, we keep trying until we make it no matter how long time it takes and how many times we need to fail before we make it come true. Thru ought time, different world pictures have sat the bar on our life standards. In the beginning we used several Gods to explain what we did not understand with the nature's different phenomenon. The world has been flat and even today there are a few that claims that the world is flat. Even though religions have been strong and world pictures has been established there has always been people seeking out the truth that has dared to question the normality norms of today in their time. It's in our nature to seek and old religions and old mentalities has hold us back thru ought time. The more we know the more we have let science take a place and paint the world. What drives us is the fact that we exist in space and the tickling thought about there is something bigger out there for us to find out. A vision of a greater purpose for us or a greater being. Nature has its own solution to our never-ending progress, the fact that we exist in universe with the sky constantly reminding us with its stars and black depth and different light phenomena. This has fueled our visions with greater purposes and a greater truth then the one we live in today, no matter where in time we are. No matter how narrow minded our world picture and normality norm has been, nature and universe has always been there to make sure we progress further. We have always been inspired by nature and universe, and thanks to our imagination we have always been taking steps further in our evolution. Thru ought time our visions of religions and world pictures has united us more and more. We have constantly been coming together as a race and today we have only two main religions that today are outdated and old. Today technology unites the world and razes barriers between us in a much faster way then before. But one thing is lacking and thru ought history we have never had a world picture or a vision that is strong enough to unite us all with a common ground and a normality norm that reflects our true nature. The two main religions do not have what it takes to unite the world even though their basic concept is basically the same. They hold us back and create worse mentalities than good the way they are today. Of course, they bring a lot of good thinking to the big masses but it's still old and outdated. There is no room for the two main religions in our future to come and its time they walk the same destiny as other has before them, they need to become mythology and history. Because of the narrow-minded way the two main religions have, and their old fashion way of thinking they are holding our progress back and they stop us from seeing the truth as it is. They have filled their purpose, and we should always be grateful for that but now it's time to move on. Our visions affect us in so many ways so it's important for us to have a vision and world picture that is up to date and in sync with our evolution. Our vision of today effect how we relate to each other and how we create goals in our lives and what we strive for in our life's. It affects our way of looking at interacting with each other. For the future we need this united world picture with great enough vision for the entire planet to come together as one, to see us existing in eternity into infinity is a must for our species to overcome the challenges of tomorrow. Up till now the world has worked just fine the way it is but we have reached the point where it's time for us to take the next step. A great vision makes all the different in the world. Today we don't have that we just live the day and try to solve our problems without any real future goal other than our own greatness in life, but no thought about our future or our future generations. Great visions make us try harder and to never give up no matter how hard it is at the moment. A great example of that is when we learned to fly for a long time, we tried out different solutions with no result but by have that strong vision we never gave up and eventually we were able to build a machine that could fly. Or when we raced about being the first at the moon, we had to do a lot of research and make a lot of progress for our self in order for that to become true. And we did succeed because the vision was big enough to never stop trying. And for our future to come we must have a strong enough vision in order for us to continue to exist. Us being caretakers and maintainers of planet earth and its nature and to exist for eternity into infinity exploring everything that universe has to offer is our only option. We must put the truth about our self on the table and start seeing us as the true alpha species we are. By having that vision and that reality we will change everything about our self we will have a much healthier view upon this world and the goals in life will be for our future and when we grow up, we will dream about contributing to our world in a greater way. Something we don't do today, today we only think about our self and what this particular life will contain with small visions about our own future.

- We should aim for the stars and pass by them. As I like to say =)

By having a united vision about our future, we will grow more equal and have a greater understanding for each other, we will live in a completely different harmony with a united world picture. Dao Buddhism world picture and vision about the human species is neutral meaning it does not exclude anyone; it involves all minorities and sees the truth about humans and their evolution. Dao Buddhism does not hold humanity back today nor in the future no matter where we are in the evolution. It does not only cover the human species but all life thru ought universe. Dao Buddhism world and universal picture will last for eternity into infinity and will never go outdated. It will allow us to advance in any direction we like and always use the strongest evolutionary engine there is, peace. Having a unified world picture and normality norm for the entire planet won't make us all the same, we will still be completely diverse in our existence just like it is today. Today we have unified pictures as well, they just don't cover the entire earth. No matter what religion or ism you belong to you have the same world picture within that religion or ism, but you are still all different in your personalities and how you live your life. But you have a common life view and a common agenda that makes you relate to each other in a much better way. The same goes for Dao Buddhism, we will still all be different from each other and live different life from each other we will just have a new view of the world and universe and a vision that will last for eternity into infinity. We will all be able to relate to each other and have a greater understanding of each other's culture and situation in the world. By uniting the world, the need for peace will come naturally, war will no longer be an option since we all live under the same foundation. Peace is thousands time stronger engine then war when it comes to progress and evolution. Dao Buddhism basic vision of our existence leaves us room to always create goals and visions about our self as great evolvers and superior beings thru ought our existence in eternity into infinity. The united vision we will live with will reflect on our everyday mentality and how we interact with each other, just like today only today we still have a tendency to alienate us from each other rather than unifying between us. All these old religions and mentalities we have today makes us live in different worlds with completely different views on our equal existence on this planet. We have to unite this planet with the vision of our self as one species, the way nature truly is. We have to live in a world picture that respect and admits that nature is diverse in its foundation just the way nature truly is. We can't live with a world picture that does not reflect the true nature the way it is like we do today. We must live in a world that provides the correct foundational understanding that there are no two humans that are the same. Just like there is no flower or snowflake that are the same. That is something the two main religions fails miserably with. The old religions we have today are narrowminded and incorrect about our true nature. Humans comes in different colors, and we are different sexes, and we are all diverse in our flora of existence. That must be the foundation of our world picture. Our vision and foundation of our self must be in accordance with our true nature, that's not the way it is today. Today we have a lot of racism and hate towards each other just because we are different, that's because we lack the basic understanding that Diversity is our true nature and also our greatest strength. We have discrimination between our sexes in different ways because of old narrow-minded mentalities about how the world should be. We are getting better at it but there is still long way to go. The world of today lack the understanding that we are equally different and that all our needs are equally important. By having diversity is our nature in our base foundation in our world picture the preconceptions between us will fade slowly away from us, we will learn in early childhood that the human species flourish and exist in a diverse flora and that is our nature to be different from each other. By having that as a part of our world picture it will sprout thru our mentality by nature and our understanding will grow vastly for each other. In order to have an equal world we must have a correct view of our true nature in our world picture. Our vision of our self will give us a completely different starting point in our life. We will grow up with the understanding of us as caretakers and maintainers of nature and that we have a responsibility to carry our existence further in eternity into infinity, that would make all the difference in the world if you compared to how we live today. For the existing generation that goes thru this change there is a lot to adjust too, and the achievement of total equality might not be something they live to experience. But they will see major improvements in the world, but this choice is not for us it's for the future generations to come. A chance to set things straight once and for all. We all have to make great effort and for some even a sacrifice. In the beginning it will be up to each individual to make a great effort to change their mentality, in the future we will grow up with the new mentality and the effort to maintain it will be easier. For some it will be harder than others. But there will be a lot in place to make this progress go faster. The new world picture will be taught in all schools and there will be all kinds of media to enforce the picture and we will all work towards this common goal. In the beginning there will be more media about all this in order to enhance the progress. TV, movie and radio producers will get a new mission to produce material that reinforces the unity for all of us. Remember that most people will already have a great understanding of what this new world means and what it will be about since this has spread from person to person before the actual choice is made globally. This change will not just be about the vision of our self and our future, and world picture but it's a change that will change our entire way of living on this planet. It will happen in many areas and as a whole, all this will help out in adjusting to the new world. Some things will happen faster than others and no matter what we will all see a great improvement of our life even if we might not live to see it all in its completion. A unified Vision is just one part of us becoming a higher form of Civilization. When we reach that point our lives will start for real, humans will become their true nature, and we will be proud of our species.

...

.

.

When we achieve time as currency it will be a complete game changer in equality. There will no longer be any differences if we are male or female, we will be working at the right place in the right time no matter who we are. There won't be any unjust balances in salary between man and woman or even between different coworkers. With time as currency, we will achieve true equality. Time is the ultimate financial eco system to have, the one we have in place today is malfunctioning and will not work for our future demands. In the future we will need to invest in time for our evolutionary progress and some of it will take a lot of time to investigate. There won't be enough money to take the necessary steps for us in the future. Time is the only valid currency when our population grow big enough. Our quota system will keep track of all the resources that we have on this planet and on other planets as well when we start to explore space more seriously. We will manage life supply by utilizing renewable resources. Time as currency belongs to a higher form of civilization and that's what we are choosing to become. People will get their motivation to contribute to the planet and the evolutionary progress and to have a healthy life as well. People that study or work will be rewarded with our quota system and get a bit better life quality. We will also celebrate peoples progress and achievements and reward them thereafter. With time as currency, we will have people working on different areas regarding to their competence and education, people will be valued for who they are and seen as a valuable member of the team they are on where all are equally important no matter the gender or color of the person doing the job. We will no longer have an unfair system but the one that we believe is best suited for the role will be chosen to perform its duties. Some projects in the future will be so large and time consuming we would not be able to do them in the world of money. And we can't have that situation. Money has played an important part in our existence, but it has played its role and are becoming obsolete and a burden to our existence. The greed today is misdirected on money and power. Greed has an ugly face that makes people do ugly things to one and each other. We will eliminate greed towards money and power and redirect greed toward evolutionary progress because greed is a powerful engine and can be utilized for good purposes. We won't lose greed just because we have time as a currency, so we need to direct it towards or main purpose to exist in eternity into infinity. When stumbling upon other intelligent life forms, money will be worthless and only time can exist as currency. Today's currency is constantly failing and will not be able to handle the future financial situations that will come. Today we have huge gaps between the wealthy society and the poorer ones. There are many countries that are underdeveloped, and they are far behind the industrial world. The world is divided in a very poor manner and it's a dysfunctional world we live in today. We suffer from having this distorted balance in the world. It weighs us down in our progress and is a major disadvantage for us to have like this on our planet. The very best solution for us is when all the countries are in the same level of existence then we have full focus on our evolutionary progress and full control over our entire planet's resources. We must build up underdeveloped countries to the same level as the rest of the world so we can bloom and flourish no matter where we are on earth. It will take a lot of effort and work of us as well as investment in resources in the beginning before we all are up to high enough standards. We are staring us blind in the world today thinking that we are making great progress the way things are, but truth is we are being very slow compared to what it would be like to have an entire world working in the same direction rather than it is now when only a small part of the world is standing for the entire progress of the world. We are crippling our self majorly by having it this way. The economy of this world can't solve the injustice between poor and rich countries. The underdeveloped countries have such a long way to go, and their undermined situation causes a lot of trouble and even civil war within the country giving them even worse possibilities to catch up with today's standard in industrial countries. All the time we have it like this we are losing efforts in progress and making our world poorer than it should be. Today we are completely missing out the big picture and we are blinded by money. The economic system we have today cannot support a world in equal existence, it's not made to keep balance in the world but to be abused and exploited by a few. While the big masses carry's the weight of a handful of men the worlds crumble in its existence growing poorer and poorer every day. The world is poor compared to a world where we have the complete population of planet earth in balance with each other, and all working to achieve further in our progress of existence. When we live in a world where time is our currency, everyone won't be doing research or inventing new solutions for us. Many people will have everyday work carrying on with their life in normal order. But that's a very important contribution as well, to make sure everything works around us and that everyone gets what they need for their everyday life. We will all have a feeling of great contribution no matter what we do because we are all equally important for this planet and our species to continue to exist and go on with our life's no matter what we do. There is no balance in the eco system of money, it does not reflect our equal being and does not properly support the true value of our efforts in work. The way we measure the value of our work effort today is insufficient and most of the time it is reflected unfair and unjust. That's the truth in workplaces but also between different countries. Money doesn't work as a system; the prices are constantly going up which results in that the people need to make more and more money. Slowly more and more people end up in poverty, and the rich people are only a handful of people. There is no sense in having money as God since it does not bring happiness only power to control other people's lives in some way. This is not a higher civilization. This is poor mentality and irresponsible way of living. With time as currency, we choose to become a higher form of civilization and take responsibility of our future. This is the next step in our evolution to become a higher form of civilization covering the entire planet and unite as one nation. We will unite with true roots of our existence that we are the human species. Today we live with no goal for the human species future, we only live for the day and making small progress in the big picture. We live aimlessly and only care about our self and our family and have no vision about us as whole picture. Most of us is happy just making a decent living making it through the day and enjoying the small parts that gives us pleasure. We have no real purpose as it is today. Hate is growing and taking a broader space because we lack a united picture where we are all equal in the eye of mother nature. Our dreams are limited by money and our progress stagnate because of that. Because of money we have a hard time to reeducate our self in order to take new paths and find new purpose of our life's. We live in different worlds today with all the different financial eco system in place for each country, what might be a citizen right in some countries are a luxury and rare thing in other countries. The way we live today we are limited to what we earn in money, some can afford a luxury lifestyle while others struggle to get by each day. Even though we are equally important in our existence. We all handle different things that's need for our population to be able to function as a whole in everyday life, from the day we are born till the day we die. People that take care of our children are majorly important for us and that's not even remotely reflected in our eco system of finance today. People that work in grocery stores are also important for us to be able to get fresh food every day to our table which is a must for us in order to live. It doesn't matter what you do as a living we are all equally important for our stimuli no matter if its mentally or physically. We all serve a purpose for each other, and we all contribute to our existence in one way or another, that should be reflected in our eco system of finance and only with time as currency we can achieve that. This is about making our self-aware about our existence in completeness to admit everyone that contributes to our lives no matter what area that is in. To acknowledge all our needs being met and satisfied as an individual in all aspects of life both physically and mentally. This is about making everyone's life count just as much, to start seeing the whole picture of our life that we exist and count just as much no matter where in life we are, and that our life is equally important no matter if you are newborn or old and retired. To admit that our wellbeing both physically and mentally thru out our entire life is important to us all. We need food, we need healthcare, we need entertainment, we need technology, we need to take care of young and old, we need it all but that's not reflected in our eco system of finance today. We need everything in order for us to be well and to be top performer of what it is we are doing. And we are all different and no one is less important than the other so we need all the variety we can get in order for us to have something for everyone. With today's eco systems of finance we are narrowing it down to only have what's popular at the moment and what's the biggest need, it is neglecting other vital parts of our everyday life. The world of money can't handle our needs and our wellbeing. Today we are depending on that we consume as much as possible in order to make as much profit as possible, the system in place does not care about the future to come and our next coming generations. We don't care about the effects our products have on nature and its supply of resources. There is no thought about making the world last as long as possible making sure we have enough to last and not deplete them prematurely. In the higher form of civilization, we take responsibility over our planet and its resources, and we take responsibility over our existents in our equal being and living. In the world of money, we can't do everything that's needed for us to handle our future problem because it costs too much money. There will be project we can't do because they are too big or take too long time and there is not money enough to do them, and if we chose to do some project that cost money it will be at cost of something else, even today we cut funds in areas in order to afford something else. We are constantly hurting ourselves by cutting funds in areas where funds are severely needed, we simply don't have enough money to take care of a country as a whole as it is today. We can't have it like that. That does not work for the future problems that will come. The future will face more advanced problems and, in more areas, than what we are used to handle today. We must take the step to become a higher form of civilization in order for us to be able to manage what the future brings us. This is the final step for as a primitive species, it's time we take the step and become self-

sufficient for real and where we take
responsibility for our existence completely
instead of just living life hoping that it will solve
by itself or by someone else. Money just isn't
good enough for us anymore, it has played its
role and are now obsolete.

- Today's world is outdated
  and old, it is time we
  welcome the future and
  the world of tomorrow. It is
  time we choose to become a
  higher form of civilization.

With time as currency, we will not have the same
problem as today, we won't have any problem
with resources as in number of employed
people. That cost will vanish completely and that
makes all the difference in the world. It will be
controlled in some manner by quota so you don't
over hire people in comparison to what works
need to be done, but it will be generous
measures in place for that. When we utilize and
invest in time, we can for real have six-hour
workdays and have two shifts working rather
than just one. We will have longer opening times
and people will be more active. In the beginning
their will only be enough people for two maybe
three shifts in some cases but when the
population reaches 15 or 20 billion or more then
we will have open twenty-four seven and the

planet will never truly sleep for real. With time as currency more people can get higher education instead of as it is today with high costs leaving us with a debt for a lifetime. Education will be a very important part of our lives; we will reeducate our self at least once in life in order to keep up with progress and today that's only possible if you live as two people together which is a major disadvantage for the ones that lives alone. Education will be equalized to work since it's about maintaining our future. With time as currency, we can have a society that always functions one hundred percent on all levels. We will manage recourses in a completely new way and making all the renewable ones available for our population at all times. We can plan and manage our resources so that there is always more than enough for not just us but our future generations as well. All we need to consider is how long time it takes to produce the product and how much we need to produce. It's all about time management. Time is all it takes. Time is the answer to our future. Time as financial eco system is another part of becoming a higher form of civilization.

...

.

One language is also an important corner stone for a higher form of civilization. When we have one world language, we will have completely new conditions for us to coexist. We will all of a sudden be able to communicate with each other all over the world and we can erase any misunderstandings we had before. We will break down barriers between each other and reach an equality between cultures that have not existed before. This will create a greater understanding for each other's differences. One language will help us unite even more and we will have a closer relation to one and other. We will have easier to compare and adjust each other's progress when we have a common tung and we will have it much easier to cooperate between continents in all areas of expertise. This is a natural step for us to take and we already got widely spread and common business language in many countries, but this is about making a statement that we are one unity planet and making sure not just a group of countries can communicate but everyone over the whole planet can communicate with each other. Today many countries have pride in their mother tung and don't want to speak another language since they feel that their language is much better than all the others, it's time to let go of that pride and commit to this change for the future and for our existence in eternity into infinity. We have to put our old tradition aside and raise with the occasion. This is not a question about excluding any language, but everyone will keep their mother tung, we will only agree upon a united world language. A language that everyone will learn from childhood just like their mother language and become bilingual by nature. We should probably go for what's most natural for everyone since choosing a too limited language will make the progress harder for everyone. No matter what the choice turns out to be it will be a choice for our future and the planet as a whole. In the future when we have used the language for a very long time, we will probably add words from our world's native languages into the world language and stop using our native language completely. But that's far ahead in the future when we have evolved for a long time. With one common language the education will be much easier to advance and make people around the world equal in knowledge. The educational material only needs to be made in one language and no misinterpretation between translations will happen. Everyone will have an up-to-date language with all the progress changes updated. We will maintain our culture by keeping our mother language and thereby nurturing our diversity for the future as well, but a new culture will grow up and take a shared place with our existing one and we will need that for our sense of unity with each other. The world language will ease up the communication in politics and in science as well as give the people of the world a completely new range off possible connections and friendships that was not possible before. We will now have networks of people that spans the entire globe and not just a few as it is today but all of us. The world language will create equality between people no matter what color or culture they come from. One language gives us the freedom to move around the world and to live and work wherever you want or are needed. As united as the species human being we must have a world language to identify our self with, it's a part of our future and it will be a part of our precent time as well. The older generations that have not learned the new world language will have a harder time then the young ones most likely but as I said before it's not only for us it's for our coming generation in the future in eternity into infinity.

...

.

We will have a fresh start and turn the calendar to year 0 again. This we do to mark and celebrate that we have finally taken the final step to a new era as a higher form of civilization and left the old primitive way of life behind us. We will also put a definitive end to both religions existence and put them into history and mythology for good. We can't have two timelines as we have today it's just a primitive way of having the world divided. We should have year 0 as a definition that we begin our new journey as a higher form of civilization and have made the decision to exist for eternity into infinity as caretakers and protectors of nature. This is a new beginning, and we need to reinforce it as much as possible. We are making history with this step in our evolution, and we need to reflect it on the world we live in today and this is the time when we set everything straight with no room for failure. We are reaching the end of our primitive existence, and we will put the old world behind us letting go of old values and disagreements. We are entering a new fresh world with us as the human species as the foundation of our existence. We are letting our history be just what it is, history. We will amend the new world picture of our self as united, and we all have one and the same foundation to stand on. We no longer need to argue about whose religion is right or not. We will leave the old world behind us with war and inflation as history. We should always remember our old world and be proud of our evolution, making sure we never strive on that erroneous path ever again. We will have year 0 again to celebrate our start on our journey in eternity into infinity and that we were able to make the final step before it was too late. This is a completely new chapter of our existence, and a new dawn will raise above the planet and the human species.

…

.

.

Dao Buddhism will be the new foundation for us here on planet earth. People will live a normal everyday life and not reflect over Dao Buddhism as the new normality norm. When Dao Buddhism is the normality norm, and a part of the world picture people will have a new mindset for their existence some stronger and others vaguer. Dao Buddhism will ease the up the differences between us and help us appreciate the diversity between each other. When we grow up with this norm, we will no longer find our diversity alien to each other. We will have a neutral and bisexual sexual orientation, and we will find beauty and attraction in both genders. We need a common baseplate to stand on in order to unite and none of the two main religions has what it takes to bring us together. Not in the past, not now and not for the future. This is about to see us as one united species, the human being and to accept that we are all one and the same in our foundation. To have this new foundation will make a big difference in how we relate to each other and coexist in a completely new way. Growing up with this norm, we will no longer find it strange or weird to be with the same sex nor will we have any hate towards this behavior. At some point of people's life, they will wonder into True soul searching and get deep into their own true self being. Dao Buddhism does not exclude anyone or anything, it will never go obsolete and never become a burden for our evolutional progress. In order to live as a higher form of civilization you need this solution in order to unite and live in harmony on this planet. The planet of today has proven for thousands of years that the way it is now can't handle and unite this world as it is today, but Dao Buddhism can. Some will go deeper into Dao Buddhism and become monks. They are searching for greater wisdom and harmony within themselves. It doesn't matter if you are male or female all can achieve the life of a monk. To have a new foundation of the world picture will slowly change how we interact with each other and for the generations that grows up with it, it will be a major difference in the society compared to what it is like today. We must be aware of how we foster our next coming generations, and we are the ones that must make the big sacrifices but it's all worth it because you are saving the future of our existence, and you are the one making it possible for us to exist in eternity into infinity.

...

.

.

True love is a mysterious state of being, Love will become more sincere in the new world. Gold diggers that only look for wealth is no longer a problem since we live in a world without money. Of course, we will still have people falling for people that are celebrity or have highly attractive positions, but love will have a more natural approach then before and people will have it easier to follow their heart now. Love is blind and it happens between the most unpredictable people sometimes. Age does not matter and sometimes old and young just find each other like everyone else does. It will be a completely new world to find love in and the whole planet is it base plate where you can find your love in any part of the world since everyone speaks the same language. It's like that a lot even today but not even close to what it will be like when you live in one united world. Love and sex will become differentiated in the new world and people will have a more active sex life with more different people. Sex will not equal love anymore but be a part of a healthy lifestyle for active people. This will be more obvious when the new world has existed for a while and the young generation grew up with this new world picture. We will see changes in lifestyle as well when we enter the new world, but a lot of people will have a hard time adjusting to the new way of life even though it will be an ordinary lifestyle in the future to come. Love will become purer and more honest toward each other, and it will also broaden between us. We will share our love with more people and have stronger bonds with each other. True truth is something we will come to appreciate more, and it will be the foundation of our world picture. We need to have things straight down in the world for the future to come. Truth is a vague concept since it will change with time and evolvement that gives our world new conditions for us to exist. We will have to keep up to date with all conditions and always make sure we have an up-to-date foundation of truth to stand on. This is a must since we will be living in a more changeable world, and we need to be as correct as possible for us to make sure we are on the right path when progressing in our evolution. In general, a more honest approach will take shape and people will become more upfront. The little lies will continue to exist, but people will tend to strive for a more honest way of life. There is no reason to lie even though some will try to make them look more interesting than they feel they are, but even that will change since we all have the same opportunity to do whatever we want to do. Lies only clouds our mind and leads to false perceptions of each other. It's better to be seen as whom you truly are rather than a fictional image of you that you have to remember and try to live up to. I know it might seem like a good idea at the moment but it's not worth being loved and appreciated for someone who you simple not are, in the long run it will leave you empty, and you will be confused over who you really are. To be loved and appreciated for someone you pretend to be doesn't do you any good in the long run, you will finally get to a place when that isn't enough, and you want to be seen for who you really are, and that you don't know because you pretended to be someone else for so long. True faith is something Dao Buddhism amends and are for the more devoted ones. Faith in Exists ancient and in the nature and in the force that is all around us. Faith in humanity and our evolutionary progress. Faith in yourself and your loved ones. Everyone has faith even if they don't perceive they have faith it's still there. Just waiting for us to amend it. Faith is a strong engine and should not be underestimated. Faith is the main tool when pathing the calibrating lifestyle and pathing in the force. In order to advance within the force your faith must be strong with the force. Dao Buddhism utilizes prayers. With one difference, we don't pray to a god, we pray with someone or something. There is no god in Dao Buddhism only pure faith in its purest form utilized in the force. True faith is about leaving the old primitive world behind where they amend old gods in order to get answers to their question and to abuse faith. In the old faith system, they pray to a god assuming someone else or something else is the solution and answer to their needs and problems. True faith is the combination of mind, heart, soul and spirit working together in harmony with each other. True faith is your guide and companion when facing the unknown and when you are alone. Faith aids us in the journey in true soul-searching when you need to get more advanced in that. True equality is something we will achieve with the new world order. People will no longer be different value depending on where they are located in the world. We will all have the same opportunity in life, and we will all be equal in value no matter race, color, culture or gender. The way we have it today where some countries are so poor they can barely make it thru the day, and they have much lower income then the rest of the world because their currency is not worth anything in relation to the rest of the world. Because of that the country has an even harder time to advance and get the country up to standard with the rest of the world.

- I said it before, and I say it again

We are damaging our self and our evolutionary progress by having it this way. We could have a so much more advanced existence today if we only had this kind of solution in place already. When we all are equal, and our opportunities are all the same for everyone in the world we will make progress in a much more advanced and faster paste then we do today. We have to start taking care of all our opportunities rather than the way it is today when we let the majority of our bright possibilities go to waste and fall into the shadow. We are neglecting and wasting brilliant minds, and we hurt our species in such a cruel way the way we live today. By living in the new world order, we are erasing all the variables that has caused the unequal world we live in today. In time there will no longer be any underdeveloped countries, but we will all be at the same level, and we will all contribute to the progress of the human species and this planet together. We will eliminate the unbalance between poverty and rich people in the old world and make everyone count just as much. There will be rewards for progress and achievements but not even close to the majorly uneven distribution of wealth that there is in the old world. The way wealth is distributed in the old world is primitive and do more damage than good to the world. We will erase these old primitive behavioral patterns about having the most money or greatest power as a competition between each other believing that we are better then all the others. And redirect greed and glory toward contribution to evolutionary progress and this planets wellbeing. There won't be any big problems in doing that change even though the existing generation will have to adjust to this new behavior. However, the upcoming generations that will grow up with this new world order will have no problem whatsoever. You have to see the big picture and realize that this step in evolution is not only about you, but also about our entire existence in eternity into infinity. True equality won't happen over a night and the gender gap will decrease over time and will be erased with the new generations that grow up with this normality norm. There will be major improvements for you as well, but the old ways will live on for a while before the new world order is completely ruling the world. True coexistence will happen with the new world order. We will all unite behind the fact that we are all one and the same species. We will admit our existence that we are part of this planet's nature just like the rest of the animals are and the rest of the nature that exist both on land and in sea. We will learn to be grateful that we have had the chance to exist as part of this planets evolution and that we are a product of this planet, and we are all children of mother earth. Earth is our true creator, and we shall always protect and caretake the planet that gave birth to us. We will accept that we are only a blip of this universe ancient and a natural progress of universe evolution. Universe does not belong to us we belong to the universe, and we are just as much part of universe that universe is part of us. We will coexist with all that universe has to offer and that goes for alien species as well. Even if we are the dominant species that exist on this planet, we have to start to coexist with the nature that's left on equal conditions. We must maintain nature and its wildlife and nurture our existence diversity among all living life forms. We are all part of mother nature's amazing flora of life and should respect what mother earth has provided to this planet. The same goes to future findings of life on other planets, we can't comprehend how advance universe is in all its glory. All the possibilities that just exist there waiting for us to discover it. Universe is so advanced there is endless of possibilities and progress to make. It's time we accept and take our universal existence seriously. We have to see our self in the bigger picture now when we have populated the entire planet and needs to start caretaking and nurture the planet as the supreme species we are here on earth.

...

.

.

The world of today is deceived by the tabu about anal sex and the normality norm that rules the world makes humanity blind to the truth. Today people don't know that the greatest orgasm pleasure is the anal orgasm and therefore they don't naturally learn how to experience anal sex. Both men and woman have the anal orgasm as their greatest pleasure point and men with the addition of the prostate gland has an even greater orgasm pleasure. Today people grow up without these facts about the straight normality norm and are shaped by media and common knowledge that the natural state of sexual being is straight. That is a lie we have been living in for thousands of years. In the new world that will change with the start from school. We will have proper sexual education teaching the truth about anal sex and anal orgasm explaining in detail how the human nerve system anatomy map is. We will also change the media on all levels to reflect the human's true sexual nature with movies and TV showing a natural state of man and women having sex with both sexes. And men preferring anal sex to get the maximum stimuli. With a common foundation and well-known fact that anal orgasm is the greatest pleasure point for both sexes the world picture will change, and the so-called hetero normality norm will die out.

Humans are truly sexual in its normality norm and their taste is bisexual. It has only been ruled out because today's norm so strongly erases the natural choice of allowing yourself to be attracted to the same sex. Only a few brave ones allow them self to be attracted to the same sex today and they are considered a minority. When it's a common understanding that you are sexual and mix with both sexes the choice will come naturally to be with both men and women for both sexes. It's understandable that a man becomes homosexual but never again straight, the man always has a reason to have anal sex because anal orgasm for man is so much greater pleasure then normal orgasm. Today's normality norm has failed for thousands of years to put something as simple as this together because of tabu. And the two main religions have done a great job to make sure we don't live in a true world. When people grow up with this understanding the sexuality will come naturally, and no one will wonder or think it's strange to be with the same sex as yourself. The world of tomorrow will look completely different to what you have seen today. Hate crimes towards sexually differences will no longer exist. We will live a mature and respectful life where everyone's sex life will improve majorly. Everyone can experience an anal orgasm both man and women and everyone can improve their sex life by open up their mind and see the truth about sexual stimuli. This is a natural step for humanity to take, we are evolving on all levels and the era of the heterosexual normality norm has come to an end.

...

.

.

We will enter a new era; an era of thousands of years of peace and war will become a memory that we will never forget. We will still need a top-notch army because we must always be prepared to defend our self-in case there will come a hostile threat from outer space. Our vision is to exist in eternity into infinity and in order to do that we can't exclude any possibility. The army will take care of hazard projects that needs extra caution and high security. They will be the first to enter new planets and reconcile that everything is safe to proceed. And in the beginning, they will be needed as long as we are divided in two worlds the new world and the old world. Their purpose is to end any hostile advancement as soon as possible and to maintain peace between the two worlds. Never to attack a peaceful opponent, we are all about defense only. Although we have an army that is kept at tip top, we will enter an era of peace that will last for thousands of years. We will become a united universe with everyone striving to find the truth about our universe existence and focus on our progress in evolution. When everything is in order and the whole planet is at equal state and in sync we will simply choose what to focus on next and nothing will be excluded. We just choose order in what to put our efforts into next and we keep track of progress of our projects. Some will take very long time and others not so long, the ones that takes long time we try to decide if we need more resources to put into that field or just maintain the progress as it is. We will live in a time of wonders and discoveries where there is no end to our possibilities. We will be able to plan our evolutionary progress over several generations making choices of what area we should make progress the next coming hundreds of years. We will gear our future the way we like and never have to worry about obstacles that will be too hard to overcome. We live in a world where we invest in time, and we will do that to one hundred percent. We will have projects that come to point where we don't have what it takes to continue its progress, but then we won't trash that project, just put it on hold until we reach enough progress or evolve in right areas for us to keep on going on that particular project. Nothing will go to waste; we will explore and discover everything there ever is to reveal. We have a whole universe to explore, and we are equipped with the most fabulous brain that can imagine and vision anything that we could ever dream of to discover. There is no end for our evolution and with the new world order we have all the time in universe to walk that path of never-ending evolutionary progress. By entering the new world order, we will be able to manage this planet with far more population than we would ever be able to with the old world. With the new world order, we can manage to grow and maintain a healthy planet for a very long time, and we will make sure we never put this planet to a premature end. We will bring life further and we will be experts in life management. We will discover ways to bring life to dead planets so we can start populating them as here on earth. At first there will be very restricted ways but remember we have all the time there ever is into eternity into infinity and that's a very long time. Eventually we will be able to recreate the natural flora and nature's own ecosystem with sweet and salt water and to bring new life to those environments. We will just need planets that has the right conditions for life to exist upon them. And we will even be able to do that on harsher environments then here on earth with all the discoveries we will do. We will populate other planets and massive space stations and expand slowly thru out universe. We will discover all the hidden secrets that hides in universe. It's just a question about time, and that we have all there ever is of it.

...

.

.

There will be no compromise in this evolutionary step, no deals to be made. No one can escape the truth as it is, and no one should be put on top of another. This is the way to proceed into the future and nothing else counts. This is about taking the step to become a higher form of civilization and there are no shortcuts to be made in order to take this step. We have to put the old primitive world behind us and grow into the role of a higher form of civilization. The new world order leaves no room for halfhearted attempts or any hassles in the formula. There is nothing to bargain with here, we are moving into a world without money and time as currency so no one can buy or bribe benefits or alter the world picture. Those days will end with the old primitive world, the days when people with money bought their happiness and controlled the world with money. This is about making a stand for the future, for the human race and for this planet continued existence. There will be rewards for everyone and not just a few selected ones. There will be no one with the ultimate power of the planet but it will be a world for the people since the people is the heart of every country. The politicians will be more of caretaker and guardians of the systems in place and the people will have the say in how things will be done. The normality norm of the old world has failed miserably with bringing this world together in an equal and just way, it is time we put that norm into history. This is the end of a world that has been corrupted and tainted by greed for money and power. The old and primitive world that has been fueling a system that gives corruption a chance to flourish and bloom all over the world. Where it has been more common in the underdeveloped countries but also exist in the industrial world. Money has been the means to put yourself above the law to be someone that has the possibility to commit crimes without any consequences. We will leave all that behind us and enter a world of equal opportunities and possibilities. People will no longer be under influence of money and can no longer be bought for favorable treatment. We won't live in a world without crimes though, crimes will take new shapes and forms and we will still need to have a police force that maintains the wellbeing of our society.

...

.

.

There is an arduous path to walk in order for this change to happen and we will see a lot of upset faces all over the world over the facts revealed in both books. But this is the natural step for us to take and we are standing at the brink of the next evolutionary step in this planet history. People will find it hard to let go of old views and perceptions of truths that people have grown up with even though they are faulty it's not easy to discover that you lived in a lie your entire life. Some of the facts are so groundbreaking that it will become a similar situation as when earth was flat and then people discovered it was round. I'm not saying this will be an easy journey but a necessary one, nevertheless. This might be a bit hard on the generations of today but it's just normal in the spirit of change. Today we have a better understanding of change, and we can make this type of adjustment, it's not foreign to us to see the world change and reshape. We have a greater understanding about evolutionary progress and how to make planet wide decisions. This is not as tricky as it sounds, we have already made merger of countries and changed financial eco system and it's all a big machinery but far from undoable and not that hard to organize when we are many countries enough. Today we have all the media we need in place in order for us to pull of all the changes needed. This was not possible before all the infrastructure was in place. We live in a time when all the possibilities are on hold because we need to take this next step. Now we progress and evolve around technology which is very good but in the big picture we are ready to take the next step and become a higher form of civilization. That will open up doors for our species to new possibilities and give us the opportunity to focus on our progress and our advancement will take new heights where there is no limit to how we evolve as a species. We will for the first time be able to plan our existence several hundred years ahead and stake out the path we want to evolve in stages so that we can monitor and change focus when needed in order to reach the goals we stake out. In this old primitive world, we don't have that kind of opportunity because there is not funds enough for that and the world isn't compatible with that kind of existence. This kind of advanced existence in the new world is not possible with the old primitive world because it requires a united world and so much time that when counted all together when everyone is cooperating all over the world and working as one, there would never ever be enough money in the universe to be able to perform this kind of evolvement. The old world does not allow us to think over generations in generational thinking. It does not provide room to plan far ahead for the future to come. The old world is primitive, and the people of that world behaves like fools, cluttering up their life around money and creating false happiness with a fool's competition in who is worth the most. People don't see each other for who they truly are but everyone is pretending to be better than they are for real, just to be more popular in a contest that is false and empty of joy and happiness. In the old, primitive world the companies care only about profit and to make as much money as possible, there is no room for what's best for our progress or evolutionary and generational thinking. Companies completely lack the ability to think on what's the best way to advance and grow and how can we provide the best service for the people since it is a cost that's not desired for the company that only cares about profit and to be as high ranked as possible in the world of finance. The best way for companies is the way that is most cost-efficient and not what is most beneficial for the rest of the world. There is a huge lack of cooperation between companies that are in the same field as each other because they compete in who gets the most money. I'm not saying that competition is not healthy because it is a necessary boost to our progress, and we will still compete with each other even though we cooperate with each other in the new world. There will be a completely different mentality in the new world between competing instances, we will share our progress with each other and spin on each other's ideas and help to improve the work we are doing. We still reward different achievements and find honor in making progress for the human species. We will encourage new ideas and people trying out new paths to explore and make sure we maintain as diverse environment as possible. Diversity truly is our greatest strength not just in the way we are but the ideas we choose to follow, and in the progress, we make in different areas. In the new world we will make sure we always are as diverse as possible because like other isms that has failure as concept with a world where everybody is the same, we will grow poorer and hurt our progress when we lose the ability to think differently. It might be a bit confusing with diversity and unity, but it's not that hard. We need a united foundation and world picture, and a united vision of the future while we need a diverse existence in our everyday life and as human species.

...

.

.

This will start slowly spreading from person to person one step at a time. I haven't really talked about this before this one the second book is done, since I have not been ready for it until now. The books will be promoted, and I will work my forces to spread the word slow and steady in the beginning, but more intense the further ahead we come. The new website is currently up and running and it's getting many visitors you will find the website in the end of the book. I strive to have this book available worldwide and for everyone to have a chance to take part of this as soon as possible. We will grow as a mass and communities will grow slowly step by step. Eventually we will reach the media and start to be seen in the bigger picture and word starts to travel around as well. This is a peaceful journey and people need the time they need in order to process all the information that has been revealed to them. It will be a bit random where it all starts for real since I don't know where this will have its foothold in the beginning. I simply have to follow the nature of its evolvement. During this entire journey the people that choose to be a part of this will play a major important role in how things will proceed. You never know who you meet or who you have in front of you when you journey, not until you choose to find out who you are dealing with. I don't know if I will live to see this day come true or if it's left for coming generation to live thru. All I know is this is a vital choice we need to make, and we must take a stand for this planet and our species in order for us to continue to exist for eternity into infinity. This is our final step as a primitive species to take in order to become a higher form of civilization. This is for all our existence future including all life upon this planet and the planet itself. This is the greatest step in human mankind history. It's no easy task but it has to start somewhere so it's time for you to take a stand for our future, it's time for you to do the greater thing in your life and make our existence a higher form of civilization. It's time for you to say yes to life and to gear this species and all life upon this planet into a future that will extend in eternity into infinity. It's time for you to make a stand for all the next coming generations to come and be a part of the ones that made it possible for them to exist in a marvelous universe. It's time for you to take a stand for true equality all over the planet and to take a stand to reveal and bury all the lies we been living in and start a fresh plate, a new leaf, a new turn of existence-

- I hereby humbly invite you to join me in my journey to a better tomorrow.

Don't be afraid, it's time to shape up and become a part of the solution rather than being a part of the problem. One human can make a change, you can make a change. The journey will be rocky, but everyone will have their own part of it in one way or another. The whole world will wake up and we will enter the new era as a higher form of civilization. It will be a new turn of the page, a new leaf, a brand-new start, a possibility to set things straight and live in a world that will spiral for eternity into infinity.

...
.

The End

- Thank you for reading my vision and the vision of Dao Buddhism.

- I sincerely hope you enjoyed reading this and that you now dare to have a greater vision of our future.

- This is the beginning of something new for both me and you.

- Welcome to the future, dear.

- May the force be with you.

Lovingly regards
Medusa Loveheart

Books by Medusa Loveheart.

1. **The Proposal** A new arrival: Dao Buddha
2. **One Unity** Now and beyond

Website

www.daobuddhism.net